EPOXY RESIN ART FOR BEGINNERS

A Step-By-Step Guide to Creating Stunning Craft Masterpieces. Unlock Your Artistic Potential with Easy-To-Follow Techniques and Inspiring Projects to Realize at Home

TAYLOR MITCHELL

TABLE OF CONTENTS

INTRODUCTION   **11**

CHAPTER 1 - FROM MATERIAL TO MAGIC: BE CAPTIVATED BY THE POWER OF EPOXY RESIN   **13**

1. THE ALCHEMY OF ART: EXPLORING THE TRANSFORMATION OF EPOXY RESIN   13

2. SYMPHONY OF COLORS: THE INCREDIBLE PALETTE OF PIGMENTS AND DYES FOR YOUR RESIN ART   15

3. THE MAGIC OF TRANSPARENCY: CREATING DEPTH AND LUMINOSITY EFFECTS WITH RESIN   17

4. RESIN AS AN EXPRESSIVE MEDIUM: EXPLORING THE CREATIVE POTENTIAL OF AN INNOVATIVE MATERIAL   18

5. THE FASCINATION OF FLOW: A GUIDE TO MANIPULATING RESIN TO CREATE UNIQUE WORKS OF ART   19

CHAPTER 2 - EXPLORE THE DEPTHS: DISCOVER THE SECRETS OF A VERSATILE AND FASCINATING MATERIAL   **21**

1. UNLIMITED VERSATILITY: THE VARIOUS APPLICATIONS OF EPOXY RESIN IN ART   21

2. A JOURNEY INTO THE HEART OF RESIN: COMPOSITION, PROPERTIES, AND ESSENTIAL CHARACTERISTICS   22

3. THE POWER OF ADHESION: TECHNIQUES FOR A LASTING UNION BETWEEN RESIN AND MATERIALS   24

4. THE ART OF MEASURING: A GUIDE TO THE CORRECT PREPARATION AND MIXING OF RESIN   25

5. BEYOND THE SURFACE: EXPLORING FINISHING AND POLISHING TECHNIQUES FOR A PROFESSIONAL EFFECT   27

CHAPTER 3 - READY TO CREATE: A GUIDE TO ESSENTIAL GETTING STARTED TOOLS AND MATERIALS   **29**

1. THE CREATOR'S EQUIPMENT: DISCOVER THE ESSENTIAL TOOLS FOR WORKING WITH RESIN   29

2. AN OASIS OF MATERIALS: EXPLORE MATERIAL OPTIONS AND FEATURES FOR YOUR RESIN ART   31

3. SET UP FOR SUCCESS: TIPS ON HOW TO ORGANIZE YOUR
WORKSPACE FOR OPTIMAL CREATIVE FLOW   32

4. FROM SAFETY TO CREATIVITY: GUIDELINES FOR PERSONAL
PROTECTION AND THE EXPLORATION OF ORIGINAL IDEAS   33

**CHAPTER 4 - ENCHANTING POURS: TECHNIQUES FOR CREATING
SUGGESTIVE EFFECTS WITH RESIN   35**

1. THE DANCE OF COLORS: EXPERIENCE THE FLUID POUR
TECHNIQUE TO CREATE ABSTRACT EFFECTS   35

2. THE ART OF INCLUSION: FIND OUT HOW TO ADD OBJECTS
AND MATERIALS INSIDE THE RESIN   36

3. THE MAGIC OF CELL TECHNIQUE: CREATING OPEN AND
CLOSED CELL EFFECTS FOR AN ORGANIC LOOK   38

4. PLAYS WITH CONTRAST: WORKING WITH COMPLEMENTARY
COLORS AND BLENDING TECHNIQUES FOR DRAMATIC EFFECTS   39

5. THE ART OF ACCIDENTALISM: EXPLOITING THE UNEXPECTED
TO CREATE UNIQUE AND EXCITING WORKS   41

**CHAPTER 5 - LAYERS OF BEAUTY: CREATING ENCHANTING ART
THROUGH THE ART OF LAYERING   43**

1. DEPTH AND DIMENSION: UNLOCKING THE SECRETS OF LAYERING
TO BRING YOUR WORKS TO LIFE   43

2. THE POWER OF LAYERS: EXPERIMENTING WITH DIFFERENT
LAYERING TECHNIQUES TO CREATE THREE-DIMENSIONAL EFFECTS   44

3. PLAY WITH TRANSPARENCY: UTILIZING TRANSLUCENT MATERIALS
TO CREATE LAYERS OF BEAUTY   45

4. THE ART OF CONTROL: MASTERING THE LAYERING PROCESS
FOR PRECISE AND ELEGANT RESULTS   46

5. THE ALLURE OF MATTE LAYERS: UNLEASHING DRAMATIC EFFECTS
WITH MATTE COVERAGE   47

**CHAPTER 6 - THE ART OF INCLUSION: FROM NATURAL INCLUSIONS
TO CUSTOMIZED CREATIONS   49**

1. TREASURES OF NATURE: UTILIZING NATURAL MATERIALS
TO CRAFT MAGICAL INCLUSIONS IN YOUR WORKS   49

2. BEYOND THE ORDINARY: EXPERIMENT WITH UNCONVENTIONAL
INCLUSIONS TO ADD A UNIQUE TOUCH TO YOUR CREATIONS   50

3. CUSTOMIZED INCLUSION: CREATE PERSONALIZED OBJECTS
TO INCLUDE IN RESIN FOR A PERSONAL TOUCH   51

4. THE ART OF BALANCE: DISCOVER HOW TO PLACE AND INCLUDE
INCLUSIONS FOR A HARMONIOUS EFFECT   52

5. CARVED CREATIONS: USE CARVING TECHNIQUES TO ENGRAVE
INCLUSIONS AND ADD PRECIOUS DETAILS   54

**CHAPTER 7 - PROJECTS THAT INSPIRE: FROM JEWELRY TO HOME
DECOR, CHOOSE YOUR STYLE   57**

1. SPARKLING JEWELRY: CREATE UNIQUE PIECES TO EXPRESS
YOUR PERSONALITY   57

2. FUNCTIONAL ART OBJECTS: CREATE HOME DECORATIONS
THAT BLEND AESTHETICS AND UTILITY   58

3. LIGHT AND COLOR: EXPERIMENT WITH BUILT-IN LIGHTS AND
PIGMENTS TO CREATE STUNNING EFFECTS   59

4. CUSTOMIZE YOUR ENVIRONMENT: IDEAS AND TIPS TO ADAPT
PROJECTS TO YOUR NEEDS   60

**CHAPTER 8 - OVERCOMING THE OBSTACLES: TIPS AND
SOLUTIONS TO AVOID COMMON RESIN PROCESSING PROBLEMS   63**

1. DEFEAT AIR BUBBLES: TECHNIQUES FOR ACHIEVING A SMOOTH
AND FLAWLESS SURFACE   63

2. ACHIEVING A FLAWLESS TRANSPARENT RESIN: PREVENTING
STAINS AND UNDESIRABLE RESIDUE   64

3. TIME AND TEMPERATURE: PRECISE MANAGEMENT OF VARIABLES
FOR OPTIMAL RESULTS   65

4. THE STICKY PROBLEM: STRATEGIES TO ADDRESS NATURAL
RESIN ADHESION   67

5. CREATIVE RESCUE: SOLUTIONS TO CORRECT MISTAKES
AND TURN THEM INTO OPPORTUNITIES   68

**CHAPTER 9 - EXPLORING NEW HORIZONS: INSPIRATION FROM
SUCCESSFUL ARTISTS AND INNOVATIVE TRENDS   69**

1. VISIONARIES OF RESIN ART: STORIES OF ARTISTS WHO
REVOLUTIONIZED THE USE OF EPOXY RESIN   69

2. ADVANCED EXPERIMENTS: EXPERIMENTAL AND INNOVATIVE
TECHNIQUES TO TAKE YOUR ART TO A NEW LEVEL   70

3. BEYOND THE RESIN: COMBINED MATERIALS AND MIXED
TECHNIQUES TO CREATE ECLECTIC AND UNIQUE WORKS   72

**CHAPTER 10 - KEEPING EXCELLENCE: GUIDE TO THE CARE AND
CONSERVATION OF RESIN WORKS**   **73**

1. MAINTAINING BEAUTY OVER TIME: TIPS FOR CLEANING,
MAINTENANCE, AND PROTECTION OF RESIN WORKS   73

2. PERFECT EXPOSURE: TIPS FOR POSITIONING AND LIGHTING
RESIN WORKS   75

3. REPAIR AND RESTORATION: STRATEGIES TO ADDRESS
ANY DAMAGE OR DEFECTS OVER TIME   76

**CHAPTER 11 - PROJECT IDEAS: START CREATING YOUR FIRST
EPOXY RESIN OBJECTS**   **77**

PROJECT 1: LAMP WITH INCORPORATED LED LIGHTS   77

PROJECT 2: COLORED EARRINGS   79

PROJECT 3: FLORAL RING   81

PROJECT 4: COASTERS   83

PROJECT 5: WALL CLOCK   85

PROJECT 6: COFFEE TABLE   87

PROJECT 7: JEWELRY PENDANT   89

PROJECT 8: PHOTO HOLDER WITH INCLUDED ELEMENTS   91

PROJECT 9: LAYERED ABSTRACT PAINTING   93

PROJECT 10: DECORATIVE TRAY   95

CONCLUSION   **97**

INTRODUCTION

Welcome to a world of magic, creativity, and boundless beauty. In this book, we invite you to immerse yourself in the fascinating and ever-evolving art of epoxy resin. Resin offers endless possibilities for artistic expression, allowing you to create unique works that capture the imagination and captivate the eye.

Whether you are an emerging artist seeking new challenges, a curious hobbyist, or an art enthusiast eager to discover new horizons, this book is designed for you. We will guide you through a captivating, step-by-step journey to explore the techniques, styles, and infinite potential that epoxy resin offers.

Together, we will delve into the fundamentals of working with resin, from acquiring essential materials to understanding proper proportions and mixtures. We will teach you techniques for achieving flawlessly smooth surfaces, blending vibrant colors, and creating distinctive effects.

However, we won't limit ourselves to just the basics. We will also delve into the art of inclusion, discovering how to incorporate natural materials and custom or unconventional objects into resin to infuse your creations with a touch of magic and originality. Furthermore, we will explore the art of balanced placement and incorporation of inclusions for visually stunning effects achieved through harmonious balance.

We will address common challenges that arise when working with resin and provide tips and solutions for overcoming them. Additionally, we will assist you in preserving the excellence of your work over time by offering guidance on caring for, maintaining, and preserving resin creations.

Get ready for a captivating journey that will transcend the boundaries of your imagination. Whether you are drawn to the sparkling beauty of resin jewelry, the limitless creativity of artwork, or the opportunity to personalize your home with unique decorations, this book serves as your essential guide for exploration, experimentation, and the creation of masterpieces.

Prepare to unlock your artistic potential, be inspired, and surprise yourself with what you can accomplish with epoxy resin. The journey begins now. Welcome to the enchanting world of resin art!

CHAPTER 1 - FROM MATERIAL TO MAGIC: BE CAPTIVATED BY THE POWER OF EPOXY RESIN

1. THE ALCHEMY OF ART: EXPLORING THE TRANSFORMATION OF EPOXY RESIN

Epoxy resin is a captivating material that, through true artistic alchemy, transforms simple chemical components into extraordinary and mesmerizing works of art.

Epoxy Resin: A Brief Introduction

Epoxy resin is a polymeric material that exists in liquid form before catalyzation. It comprises two primary components: the resin and the catalyst. When combined, these components initiate a chemical reaction that leads to the resin's polymerization and solidification, resulting in a resilient and transparent material. Epoxy resin offers boundless creative possibilities due to its versatility and unique properties.

The Magic of Catalyzation: Transforming the Resin

Catalyzation is the pivotal process that enables epoxy resin to transform into a solid and durable substance. During catalyzation, the catalyst activates the chemical reaction that triggers resin polymerization. This process can be controlled to modulate the rate of curing and achieve desired effects. It is the artist's role to comprehend and master catalyzation in order to unleash the full creative potential of epoxy resin.

The Role of the Artist: Manipulating and Shaping the Resin

In the process of transforming epoxy resin, the artist plays a fundamental role. It is the artist who decides how to manipulate and shape the resin to achieve the desired effect. The choice of tools and application techniques influences the final outcome. Artists can explore the flow of resin, create layers, incorporate objects, and employ various techniques to express their creativity and produce unique works of art.

The Exploration of Transformation: Creative Techniques and Approaches

Numerous techniques and creative approaches exist to maximize the transformative power of epoxy resin. These include fluid pouring, layering, the inclusion of materials and objects, and the use of pigments and colors, among others. Each technique opens doors to extraordinary effects and limitless possibilities.

Fluid Pouring: The Dance of Colors

Fluid pouring is one of the most captivating techniques in resin work. It enables the creation of abstract pieces with fluid movements and harmoniously blended colors. Techniques such as free pouring and "Dirty Pour" are employed to achieve intriguing and distinctive effects.

Layering: Depth and Dimension

Layering is an art form that allows for the creation of three-dimensional works with immersive depth. By overlaying layers of colored and transparent resin, captivating effects of depth, transparency, and three-dimensionality can be achieved.

Inclusion of Materials and Objects: Beyond the Ordinary

The inclusion of materials and objects enhances the fascination of resin works. Incorporating dried flowers, leaves, shells, pearls, and other elements adds a touch of originality and personality to creations. Strategic placement within the resin is key to achieving stunning results, and we will provide tips and guidance in this regard.

Using Pigments and Colors: Enhancing Artistic Expression

Pigments and colors are essential tools for artists working with epoxy resin. By employing translucent, opaque pigments, and vibrant colors, artistic expression can be elevated, resulting in captivating works of art. We will offer advice on how to mix and use these pigments and colors to create light, shadow, and gradient effects.

Experimentation and Innovation: Beyond the Boundaries of Resin

Working with epoxy resin allows for experimentation and innovation. Artists can combine resin with various materials such as wood, metal, fabrics, and even recycled materials, resulting in eclectic and unique artworks. We will ignite sparks of innovation, encouraging artists to think beyond conventional boundaries and create works that astonish and inspire.

2. SYMPHONY OF COLORS: THE INCREDIBLE PALETTE OF PIGMENTS AND DYES FOR YOUR RESIN ART

Epoxy resin opens up a world of creative possibilities, and one of its most captivating aspects is the vast range of colors available to breathe life into your artwork. From vibrant shades to subtle hues, you will discover how pigments and dyes can transform your creations into chromatic masterpieces.

Choosing Pigments: Exploring the Options

• Powder Pigments: These pigments offer a wide array of colors and enable you to create stunning effects. We will delve into the various types of powder pigments available and provide practical tips for their proper use.

• Tints and Dyes: Resin-specific tints and dyes provide convenient solutions for coloring resin. We will explore how to utilize these options to achieve vibrant and uniform results.

• Special Effects: We will also unveil special pigments and dyes that allow you to create unique effects, such as metallic, iridescent, or fluorescent finishes. Our tips will guide you on making the most of these options to add a magical touch to your artwork.

The Art of Blending: Creating Your Own Unique Shade

• Mixing Primary Colors: You will learn the art of combining primary colors to create a broad spectrum of custom hues and shades. We will provide tips on achieving consistent and reproducible results.

• Creating Transition Effects: We will guide you through the technique of gradual blending to achieve smooth color transitions. Discover how to create captivating gradients and background effects using advanced blending techniques.

Exploring Color Combinations: From Harmony to Contrast

• Complementary Colors: You will uncover the power of using complementary colors to create dynamic contrasts and enhance the visual impact of your resin works.

• Hue Harmony: We will explore the use of similar or related hues to achieve visual harmony and a sense of cohesion in your artwork.

• Experimenting with Juxtaposition: We encourage you to embark on bold and unconventional color combinations to create truly unique and striking pieces.

Coloring Techniques: Practical Tips for Applying Colors

• Basic Coloring: We will guide you through the process of applying basic colors to epoxy resin, illustrating best practices for achieving even distribution and a smooth finish.

• Color Layers: Learn how to create depth and dimension by layering colors onto resin. We will share techniques for achieving transparency effects, gradients, and vibrant details.

• Special Effects: Dive into advanced techniques such as using translucent pigments to create captivating light and shadow effects, incorporating pigments with varying densities for movement effects, and more.

The Psychology of Colors: Communicating and Evoking Emotions through Color Choice

• Meaning of Colors: Explore the meanings and emotional associations of different colors, empowering you to use color as a powerful tool for conveying messages and eliciting specific reactions from your audience.

• Contexts and Applications: We will discuss the implications of color in specific contexts, such as decorative art, jewelry, or commissioned artwork, offering suggestions on adapting color choices based on the context and personal preferences.

3. THE MAGIC OF TRANSPARENCY: CREATING DEPTH AND LUMINOSITY EFFECTS WITH RESIN

Transparency is a fascinating aspect of epoxy resin, and you will discover techniques to harness the translucent properties of resin and create mesmerizing artworks that appear immersed in a magical dimension.

Transparent Epoxy Resin: A Unique Material

• We will describe the distinctive characteristics of transparent epoxy resin and explore its artistic potential.

• An explanation of the optical properties that give resin its transparency and luster.

Creating Depth with Resin Layers

• We will delve into techniques for creating depth effects by layering transparent resin.

• Discover how colors, pigments, or inclusions can accentuate the sense of depth in your creations.

Working with Transparent Inclusions

• Explore the incorporation of transparent inclusions such as gems, dried flowers, leaves, or other materials into resin.

• Learn techniques for strategically placing and securing inclusions to achieve optimal aesthetic effects.

Luminous Effects with Transparent Resin

• Dive into techniques for creating vibrant and radiant effects using transparent resin.

• Discover how built-in lights or LEDs can illuminate resin artworks, enhancing their brightness.

Transparency and Material Combination

• Gain insights into the combined use of transparent resin with other materials like wood, metal, or textiles

• Receive suggestions on how to create captivating synergies between the transparency of resin and the textures of other materials.

4. RESIN AS AN EXPRESSIVE MEDIUM: EXPLORING THE CREATIVE POTENTIAL OF AN INNOVATIVE MATERIAL

Epoxy resin offers a wide range of creative possibilities for artists of all skill levels. Beyond its versatility and durability, this captivating material provides an opportunity for experimenting with new techniques and creating unparalleled works of art.

A Versatile Artistic Language

Epoxy resin can be regarded as a distinct artistic language, enabling the expression of emotions, concepts, and visions in a visual and tactile manner. Its transparent and smooth nature allows for the creation of luminous effects and depth, resulting in artworks that capture attention and stimulate the imagination.

The Creation of Three-Dimensional Works

Through its ability to harden into a solid and resilient state, epoxy resin allows for the creation of three-dimensional works that stand out for their structure and form. Artists can mold resin into various shapes and employ different techniques to achieve unique outcomes. Resin can be cast in molds, shaped by hand, or layered to create captivating three-dimensional compositions.

Experimentation with Special Effects and Textures

Epoxy resin invites experimentation with a diverse range of special effects and textures. Artists can utilize additional pigments, dyes, inks, and materials to achieve marble, stone, smoke, galaxy, and various other effects. The resin can be manipulated and worked with specific tools and techniques to achieve intriguing and distinctive textures.

Integration of Decorative Elements

An additional captivating aspect of epoxy resin is the integration of decorative elements within artworks. This may involve incorporating objects, inclusions, photographs, fabrics, or any other elements that contribute further meaning and depth to the work.

Exploration of Colors and Light Effects

Epoxy resin offers abundant possibilities for exploring color and light effects in artworks. Artists can utilize pigments, dyes, and tints to create a diverse range of shades. Transparent resin intensifies the vibrancy of pigments and generates depth and luminosity effects that captivate the viewer's eye.

Emotional Expression and Narrative

Epoxy resin empowers artists to express emotions and convey narratives through their creations. By employing shapes, colors, textures, and decorative elements, artists can construct compositions that evoke sensations and convey messages. Resin becomes a medium for narrating stories, capturing moments, and reflecting upon human experiences.

Art as a Tactile Experience

A unique characteristic of epoxy resin is its tactile nature. Artworks crafted from this material beckon observers to engage with them through the sense of touch. The smooth, glossy surface of resin entices exploration, inviting observers to feel its texture and immerse themselves in a richer and more tactile artistic experience.

5. THE FASCINATION OF FLOW: A GUIDE TO MANIPULATING RESIN TO CREATE UNIQUE WORKS OF ART

Handling epoxy resin is a captivating process that requires skill and creativity. You will discover the techniques and strategies for creating one-of-a-kind works of art by controlling the flow of resin.

Flow as a Creative Tool

The flow of resin is one of the defining characteristics of resin art. Knowing and understanding how resin moves and spreads is essential to fully harness its creative potential and create unique and intriguing effects in our artworks.

Controlled Pours: Creating Fluid Compositions

Controlled pours are widely used techniques in resin art. This method allows you to guide the flow of resin in specific directions, resulting in fluid and dynamic compositions.

Marbling Effects: Creating Movement and Depth

Marbling is an effective technique for adding movement and depth to resin artwork. This technique involves strategically mixing different colors to achieve an effect similar to the veins found in marble.

Creating Two-Dimensional and Three-Dimensional Flows

In resin art, you can create both two-dimensional and three-dimensional flows. Two-dimensional flows develop on a flat surface, while three-dimensional flows extend more significantly, creating relief and dimension effects.

Flow Control: Advanced Techniques

Flow control requires experience and skill in resin art. We will explore advanced techniques for flow control, such as using masking, layer separations, and applying resin in a controlled manner. These techniques enable you to create complex shapes, separate elements within your work, and achieve precise and accurate results.

Creative Experiments: Pushing the Boundaries of Flow

As we learn the basics of flow control, it's important to leave room for experimentation and creativity. From free pouring techniques to bold color combinations, we will dive into exploring the boundaries of resin flow and the endless creative possibilities it offers.

Resolving Common Problems: Managing Unwanted Flow and Achieving Optimal Control

While resin flow can be fascinating, it can also pose challenges and problems. You will learn how to resolve common issues related to unwanted resin flow, such as leaks, air bubbles, and irregular flow. We will also provide tips and strategies for achieving optimal flow control during the resin manipulation process.

CHAPTER 2 - EXPLORE THE DEPTHS: DISCOVER THE SECRETS OF A VERSATILE AND FASCINATING MATERIAL

1. UNLIMITED VERSATILITY: THE VARIOUS APPLICATIONS OF EPOXY RESIN IN ART

Epoxy resin is an incredibly versatile material that offers endless creative possibilities in the field of art. From abstract creations to functional works, epoxy resin provides a fertile ground for artistic expression. It can be utilized in various artistic disciplines, including painting, sculpture, jewelry making, home decor, and more. With its properties of transparency, durability, and resistance, epoxy resin lends itself to a wide range of techniques and artistic styles.

Painting and Abstract Art: Epoxy resin enables artists to create abstract works of art with effects of depth, transparency, and brilliance. Pigments and colors can be mixed into the resin to achieve a wide range of shades and hues, allowing artists to express their creativity and artistic vision.

Sculpting and Three-Dimensional Shapes: Epoxy resin allows for the creation of sculptures and three-dimensional shapes with exceptional precision and durability. Its ability to harden and maintain the desired shape enables artists to shape and mold resin into visually striking three-dimensional works of art.

Jewelry and Accessories: Epoxy resin is an ideal material for crafting unique jewelry and accessories. With its transparency and glossy properties, resin can be used to encapsulate objects, create inlaid jewelry, pendants, earrings, and much more. Artists can experiment with materials, colors, and shapes to create highly artistic and personalized pieces.

Home Decoration: Epoxy resin can be employed to fabricate decorative items for the home, such as coffee tables, vases, lamps, and picture frames. Utilizing its transparency and resistance properties, resin can be shaped and layered to produce distinctive and personalized pieces that add a touch of elegance and originality to any environment.

2. A JOURNEY INTO THE HEART OF RESIN: COMPOSITION, PROPERTIES, AND ESSENTIAL CHARACTERISTICS

To truly comprehend the potential of epoxy resin, it is crucial to embark on a journey into its core, exploring its composition, properties, and essential characteristics.

Composition of Epoxy Resin

Epoxy resin is comprised of two main components: the resin and the catalyst. The resin is typically a viscous liquid, while the catalyst initiates the chemical reaction of polymerization. When these two components are combined, the resin undergoes a process of hardening, transitioning from a liquid to a solid state.

Properties of Epoxy Resin

Epoxy resin possesses several properties that render it unique and versatile in the realm of art. One of its primary characteristics is its crystalline transparency, enabling the creation of luminous artworks. Additionally, epoxy resin exhibits resistance to external factors such as humidity, oxidation, and UV rays, making it suitable for outdoor or brightly lit displays. Furthermore, it can be easily colored using pigments and dyes, offering a wide range of creative possibilities.

Essential Characteristics of Epoxy Resin

Alongside its properties, epoxy resin possesses several essential characteristics that are vital to understand in order to maximize its potential. One such characteristic is workability time, referring to the duration available for manipulating the resin before the hardening process commences. Familiarizing oneself with the resin's pot life is crucial for planning and executing desired techniques without encountering issues.

Another significant feature is the viscosity of the resin, which may vary depending on the brand and formulation. Viscosity affects the ease of application and the ability to achieve specific effects. Different epoxy resins with varying viscosities are available to cater to diverse artistic requirements.

Mechanical resistance is a critical aspect to consider. Cured epoxy resin is generally resistant to impact, scratches, and deformation, although its specific level of resistance may vary based on the formulation and curing process.

Epoxy resin's capability to create a smooth and polished surface upon curing is a noteworthy characteristic. This makes it suitable for crafting tables, countertops, jewelry, and other creations that demand a high-quality finish. Epoxy resin can be sanded, polished, and refined to achieve a glossy, flawless surface.

In addition to its smooth finish, epoxy resin also enables the creation of three-dimensional effects. By adding successive layers of epoxy resin, it is possible to achieve reliefs, interlocking patterns, and transparencies that lend depth and dimension to artworks. This three-dimensional versatility presents endless creative opportunities, allowing for the creation of unique and personalized pieces.

Chemical resistance is another important attribute of epoxy resin. Once fully cured, the resin becomes resistant to many chemicals, including solvents, oils, and weak acids. This means that artwork made with epoxy resin can be protected from damage caused by such chemicals.

Considering the working temperatures of epoxy resin is also vital. Some resins require specific temperatures for optimal mixing and curing. It is important to adhere to the manufacturer's instructions to ensure proper handling and achieve high-quality results.

Lastly, safety is a crucial aspect when working with epoxy resin. It is essential to use protective gear such as gloves, goggles, and respiratory masks when handling and working with the resin. Additionally, it is important to ensure adequate ventilation in the workspace to prevent inhalation of harmful fumes.

3. THE POWER OF ADHESION: TECHNIQUES FOR A LASTING UNION BETWEEN RESIN AND MATERIALS

Epoxy resin offers strong bonding power, which allows it to be permanently bonded with other materials. This feature is essential for creating resin works of art that are resistant and stable over time.

Let's look at some key techniques to achieve effective adhesion:

Surface Preparation: Before bonding epoxy to other materials, it is essential to thoroughly prepare the surfaces. Make sure they are clean, dry, and free from dust, oils, or substances that could impair adhesion. Use isopropyl alcohol or a specialized cleaner to effectively clean the surfaces.

Roughness and Micro-engravings: To improve the adhesion between the epoxy resin and the base material, slight roughness can be created on the surface. This can be achieved through micro-engraving or using fine grit sandpaper. The roughness provides a greater contact area for adhesion and promotes a better seal.

Using Primer: In some cases, applying a primer or anchoring agent can improve the adhesion between the epoxy resin and the base material. The primer creates an anchoring layer that facilitates adhesion and prevents detachment over time. Make sure to use a primer that is compatible with both materials involved.

Thorough Mixing: Another crucial aspect of ensuring a solid bond is the correct mixing of the epoxy resin. Follow the manufacturer's instructions carefully regarding the proportion and mixing time. Insufficient or incorrect mixing could compromise adhesion and cause problems in the final result.

Pressure and Clamping: After applying the epoxy to the base material, apply light pressure or use clamping devices to hold the surfaces together during the curing process. This helps ensure close and even contact between the materials, improving adhesion.

Proper Cure Time: Follow the recommended cure time for epoxy resin. The full cure time will allow the resin to cure and develop a strong bond with the base material. Avoid subjecting the treated material to excessive stresses or loads during the curing period, as this may compromise adhesion.

Adhesion Testing: Preliminary adhesion testing is recommended before using epoxy on more complex projects. Apply a small amount of resin to the surface of the base material and allow it to cure. Next, perform tensile or flex tests to verify the effectiveness of the adhesion. This will give you an indication of the strength of the bond and allow you to make any necessary improvements.

Material Considerations: Take into account the nature of the base material you intend to work with. Some materials may require specific treatments or the use of special primers or adhesives to ensure optimal adhesion with the epoxy resin. For example, materials such as plastic, metal, or wood may require a different approach to achieve good adhesion.

Maintenance and Storage: Once your epoxy resin project is complete, it is important to take the right precautions to maintain adhesion over time. Avoid exposure to extreme temperatures, humidity, and harsh chemicals that may affect adhesion. Also, be sure to clean and store your artwork properly to preserve its beauty and longevity.

4. THE ART OF MEASURING: A GUIDE TO THE CORRECT PREPARATION AND MIXING OF RESIN

Measuring and properly preparing your epoxy resin is vital to achieving quality results in your artwork. Here are some important points to consider:

Safety and Protection: Before you start working with epoxy resin, make sure you are wearing the proper protective equipment, such as latex gloves, goggles, and a respiratory mask. Epoxy resin can be irritating to the skin and eyes, so it's important to protect yourself when handling it.

Accurate Measurement: Use an accurate measuring system to correctly measure the epoxy resin and hardener. You can use precision scales or measure the required quantities using measuring cups or cylinders. Follow the manufacturer's instructions carefully to determine the correct mixing ratio between resin and catalyst.

Homogeneous Mixing: After measuring the resin and catalyst, mix them thoroughly to obtain a homogeneous mixture. Use a mixing tool, such as a spatula or wooden stick, and mix firmly and continuously.

Be sure to scrape the sides and bottom of the container to ensure thorough mixing.

Processing Time: Epoxy resin has a limited processing time, so it's important to be aware of the time available to work with the material. Read the manufacturer's instructions carefully to learn the specific working time for the resin you are using. Make sure you plan your work so you can complete your pouring, handling, and finishing tasks before your working time runs out.

Temperature Control: Ambient temperature can affect the working time and curing process of epoxy resin. Make sure you work in an area with a suitable and controlled temperature. Avoid working in extreme heat and humidity, as this can speed up the curing process and make the resin difficult to work with.

Preparation of the Substrate: Before pouring the resin onto the work surface, adequately prepare the substrate. Ensure the substrate is clean, free from dust, grease, or other contaminants that could affect resin adhesion. You can clean the surface with isopropyl alcohol or a mild detergent. Also, seal any cracks or pores in the substrate with a resin-compatible primer or sealer.

Pouring and Leveling: Pour the resin onto the prepared work surface in an even and controlled manner. Make sure you distribute it evenly to avoid the formation of air bubbles. Use a spatula or brush to level the resin and create the desired effects, such as translucent layers or decorative object inclusions.

Cure and Curing: After pouring, cover the work with a lid or bell jar to protect it from dust and contaminants. Allow the resin to harden for the time specified by the manufacturer. Avoid touching or disturbing the resin during the curing process to ensure a smooth and even surface.

Finishing and Sanding: Once the resin has completely hardened, proceed with finishing and sanding the artwork. Use fine-grit sandpaper or abrasive cloths to smooth the surface of the resin and remove any blemishes or irregularities. Afterwards, you can polish the surface to achieve a shiny and reflective effect.

Protection and Preservation: After finishing, protect and preserve your artwork. You can apply a layer of clear protective varnish to maintain the shine and durability. Be sure to use a resin-compatible varnish and follow the manufacturer's instructions for proper application.

5. BEYOND THE SURFACE: EXPLORING FINISHING AND POLISHING TECHNIQUES FOR A PROFESSIONAL EFFECT

Once the epoxy resin has been worked on, it is essential to pay attention to finishing and polishing to obtain a professional result. You will learn some finishing and polishing techniques that will help enhance the look and shine of your resin work.

Sanding: Sanding is the first step in achieving a smooth and uniform surface. Use progressively finer grit sandpaper to smooth out any irregularities, imperfections, or marks on the resin surface. Start with a coarser grit, such as 120 or 220, and work your way up to finer grits, such as 400, 800, and 1200. Remember to keep the sandpaper wet while sanding to avoid heat build-up and to achieve a smoother surface.

Wet Polishing: After sanding, proceed with wet polishing to further enhance the surface's brightness. Use a resin-specific polishing paste and apply it to the surface with a soft cloth or damp sponge. Make circular and continuous movements to evenly distribute the paste on the resin. Continue buffing until you achieve your desired level of shine. Remember to thoroughly clean the surface of any residual paste after polishing.

Polishing with a Polisher: For an even higher level of polish, you can use an electric polisher. Use a resin-specific polishing pad or disc and apply polishing paste to the surface. Adjust the polisher's speed according to the manufacturer's recommendations and use slow, controlled movements to achieve an even polish. Thoroughly clean the surface of any residual paste after polishing.

Surface Protection: Once the polishing is complete, apply a surface protector to preserve the shiny appearance and protect the resin over time. There are several options available, such as clear protective varnishes or resin sprays. Make sure to choose a product that is compatible with the resin and carefully follow the manufacturer's instructions for application.

Final Details: For an even more professional effect, pay attention to the final details. Carefully inspect the surface for any imperfections or marks and correct them if necessary. Thoroughly clean your resin work to remove any dust or dirt that may have accumulated during the finishing process. Use a clean, soft cloth dipped in isopropyl alcohol to gently wipe the surface.

Special Effects: If you want to add a special touch to your resin artwork, experiment with special effects. You can embed pigments, glitter powders, or materials such as dried flowers, leaves, or decorative items into the resin before curing to create unique and interesting effects. Follow the manufacturer's instructions for adding such items and strategically place them to achieve the desired effect.

Maintenance: To maintain the beauty and durability of your resin artwork, proper maintenance is important. Avoid direct exposure to intense sunlight and excessive heat, as they may cause fading or warping of the resin over time. Periodically wipe the surface with a clean, soft cloth to remove any accumulated dust or dirt. If necessary, apply a new layer of surface protector to preserve its original appearance.

CHAPTER 3 - READY TO CREATE: A GUIDE TO ESSENTIAL GETTING STARTED TOOLS AND MATERIALS

1. THE CREATOR'S EQUIPMENT: DISCOVER THE ESSENTIAL TOOLS FOR WORKING WITH RESIN

When venturing into the wonderful world of epoxy resin, it is crucial to be well-prepared with the right tools to ensure quality results and facilitate the creative process. From basic equipment to more advanced options, let's explore how these tools can impact your artistic work's experience and final outcome.

Well-Equipped Work Table

A suitable workbench serves as the foundation for any resin project. Ensure you have an adequate, sturdy, and well-lit space. The table should offer sufficient room to accommodate the necessary tools and materials, with a dedicated area for resin mixing. Use a smooth and easy-to-clean surface, preferably covered with plastic wrap or waxed paper to protect against resin spills.

Precision Balance

Accurate measurement of resin components is crucial for reliable results. Investing in a precision balance enables you to precisely measure the epoxy resin and its hardener, following the recommended proportions provided by the manufacturer.

Measuring Cups and Containers

Graduated cups and containers are essential for proper resin mixing. Acquire a set of various-sized measuring cups, preferably transparent plastic ones for easy reading. Additionally, heavy-duty plastic mixing containers are ideal for combining the resin and hardener. Avoid using paper or metal containers as they may react with the resin and compromise its quality.

Palettes and Spatulas

A rigid plastic scoop or sheet is useful for pouring resin and mixing pigments. Use a non-porous surface that is easy to clean and does not react with the resin.

Flexible plastic spatulas are perfect for scraping the mixing container and spreading resin evenly on the work surface.

Flame Gun or Gas Torch

A flame gun or gas torch is an indispensable tool for eliminating air bubbles that form during epoxy mixing. These bubbles can affect the final appearance of your project. With an adjustable flame, gently pass the flame gun or gas torch over the resin surface to remove air bubbles and achieve a smooth, clear finish.

Protection Mask and Gloves

Safety is very important when working with epoxy resin. Always wear a protective mask to prevent inhaling the toxic vapors released by the resin and hardener. Additionally, use nitrile gloves to safeguard your hands from resin and potential skin irritation. Ensure the mask is specifically designed for chemical work and offers adequate protection.

Sandpaper and Sanding Tools

Various grits of sandpaper are essential for the smoothing phase of hardened resin. After the resin has cured, you may need to sand the surfaces to eliminate imperfections, bubbles, or excess material. Start with fine-grit sandpaper for initial sanding and progress to finer grits for a smooth, high-gloss finish. It may also be helpful to have other sanding tools, such as scrapers and abrasive sponges, for achieving precise results.

Protective and Cleaning Measures

When working with epoxy resin, it's crucial to protect your surroundings and make cleanup easier. Cover your work table with a plastic drop cloth or waxed paper to prevent resin from adhering to the surface. Keep damp cloths or wipes readily available to clean up resin spills before they solidify.

2. AN OASIS OF MATERIALS: EXPLORE MATERIAL OPTIONS AND FEATURES FOR YOUR RESIN ART

When creating art with resin, using the right materials can significantly impact the final result. From decorative inclusions to casting bases, we will explore the available options and their characteristics. By experimenting with different materials, you can enrich your creations with unique textures, colors, and effects.

Decorative Inclusions

Decorative inclusions are objects or materials that are incorporated into resin to add visual interest and dimension to your artwork. You can utilize a variety of inclusions, such as dried flowers, leaves, wood chips, shells, stones, pearls, metal pieces, and more. Ensure that the inclusions are clean, dry, and the appropriate size for your project. Place the inclusions on the resin surface or create a cast around them for stunning effects.

Pigments and Dyes

Pigments and dyes are used to color the resin and create captivating visual effects. There are several options available, including powder pigments, liquid dyes, or pigment pastes. You can directly mix pigments into the resin to achieve vibrant colors or create shades and transparencies. Experiment with different combinations to discover the desired color and develop your unique style.

Casting Bases

Casting bases serve as surfaces or objects on which you pour resin to create your artwork. You have various options for bases, such as canvas, wood, ceramic, glass, plexiglass, or even three-dimensional objects. Ensure that the base is clean, free of dust, and properly prepared to receive the resin. Additionally, you can create custom bases using molds or structures made from silicone or other suitable materials.

Protective Finishes

Once the resin has hardened, it is advisable to apply a protective finish to preserve your artwork over time. Clear coats or resin top coats can be used to provide extra protection and a glossy finish to the surface. Follow the manufacturer's instructions carefully for the application process, and allow the protective finish to dry completely before handling or displaying the artwork.

3. SET UP FOR SUCCESS: TIPS ON HOW TO ORGANIZE YOUR WORKSPACE FOR OPTIMAL CREATIVE FLOW

Creating an organized and well-structured work environment is essential to ensure optimal creative flow and maximize your resin art productivity. A well-organized environment allows you to have everything you need close at hand and work efficiently, avoiding distractions and wasted time. Here are some tips on how to organize your workspace:

Optimize the Available Space

Consider the size of your workspace and optimize it as best as possible. Utilize nooks and crannies to add shelves or hanging items, providing more room to store tools, materials, and work in progress. Use clear or labeled containers to keep everything organized and easily accessible.

Create Functional Zones

Divide your workspace into functional zones based on different activities you perform. For example, have an area dedicated to measuring and mixing resin, another for preparing molds or surfaces, and a separate area for finishing and polishing artwork. Arrange tools and materials logically for easy access.

Use Containers and Organizers

Invest in bins, boxes, or drawers to keep your workspace neat. Utilize trays or tubs with compartments to store small items like pigments, brushes, spatulas, and accessories. Clear organizers are especially useful as they allow you to see the contents without opening them.

Label and Document

Label all bins, boxes, and drawers for instant identification. This will help you quickly find what you need and maintain long-term workspace organization. Additionally, keep track of materials, tools, and techniques used for each project, enabling replication of successful creations and learning from mistakes.

Maintain Cleanliness and Safety

Cleanliness and safety are paramount in your workspace. Regularly clean tools and work surfaces to avoid contamination or unwanted residue on the resin. Use surface protectors, such as silicone mats or plastic sheets, to prevent damage or stains during resin-working activities.

Furthermore, adhere to necessary safety measures when working with epoxy resin. Always wear personal protective equipment such as gloves, goggles, and masks to avoid direct contact with the resin and exposure to harmful vapors. Ensure good ventilation in your work area or use extraction devices as needed.

Create an Inspiring Environment

Lastly, create an environment that inspires and stimulates your creativity. Add decorations, artwork, or objects that you find motivating during the creative process. Customize your workspace to match your aesthetic and artistic style. A pleasant and inspiring environment can help maintain passion and creativity while working with resin.

4. FROM SAFETY TO CREATIVITY: GUIDELINES FOR PERSONAL PROTECTION AND THE EXPLORATION OF ORIGINAL IDEAS

Safety Priority

Before diving into creativity, it is essential to understand the importance of personal protection when working with epoxy resin. Following these safety guidelines will help you perform your art safely and efficiently:

• Always prioritize safety by wearing protective gloves, goggles, and masks for eye and respiratory protection.

• Work in a well-ventilated area or use a proper ventilation system to avoid inhaling harmful vapors.

• Avoid direct contact with the resin on your skin. If contact occurs, wash it immediately with soap and water.

• Maintain thorough cleaning of your tools and work surfaces to prevent unwanted contamination.

• Store the chemical materials used in resin processing out of the reach of children and pets.

Explore Your Creativity

• Experiment with different materials: Besides resin, explore the use of other materials such as wood, metals, stones, fabrics, or found objects. Combining different materials can add depth and interest to your resin creations.

• Develop a personal style: Try to define your own unique artistic style that distinguishes you from others. Experiment with various techniques, colors, and shapes to establish your signature style.

• Make your art functional: Epoxy resin can be used to create not only decorative artwork but also functional items like jewelry, home accessories, and furniture. Utilize the versatile characteristics of resin to produce pieces that combine aesthetics and utility.

• Experiment with transparency: Transparent epoxy resin offers endless creative possibilities. Play with transparency, object inclusion, layering, and depth effects to create unique and stunning visual effects.

• Document your creative process: Keep a record of your experiments, discoveries, and inspirations. Maintain an art journal or take photos during the process to visually document your creative journey.

• Challenge yourself: Continually seek new artistic challenges. Learn new techniques, try different materials, and take on more complex projects. Embracing challenges will help you grow as an artist and explore new creative horizons.

Useful Resources

• Online community: Join groups and online communities of artists working with epoxy resin. These forums provide a space to share experiences, ask questions, and receive support from fellow community members.

• Fairs and art shows: Attend fairs and art shows specializing in epoxy resin art. These events allow you to discover new trends, meet renowned artists, and find inspiration.

• Art supply store: Visit specialty art supply stores that offer a wide selection of high-quality epoxies, pigments, paints, molds, tools, and art materials.

• Specialty websites and blogs: Explore websites and blogs dedicated to epoxy resin art. These resources provide informative articles, tutorials, product reviews, and creative ideas to enhance your artistic skills.

Utilize these resources to expand your knowledge, seek advice, and connect with the art community. Remember that creativity is a journey of continuous growth, so keep learning, exploring, and experimenting to achieve increasingly satisfying results.

CHAPTER 4 - ENCHANTING POURS: TECHNIQUES FOR CREATING SUGGESTIVE EFFECTS WITH RESIN

1. THE DANCE OF COLORS: EXPERIENCE THE FLUID POUR TECHNIQUE TO CREATE ABSTRACT EFFECTS

The fluid pour technique is one of the most fascinating and expressive methods when working with epoxy resin. This technique allows you to create unique artistic compositions in which colors blend and move in a mesmerizing dance on the surface.

Here's a step-by-step guide to experimenting with the fluid pour technique:

1. Material Preparation: Ensure that you have all the necessary tools and materials ready. You will need clear epoxy, dyes or pigments, mixing cups, spatulas, paintbrushes or pipettes, and a protected work surface.

2. Resin Preparation: Thoroughly mix the epoxy resin according to the manufacturer's instructions. Ensure that you achieve a smooth, bubble-free mixture.

3. Adding Colors: Divide the resin into several mixing cups and add your preferred colorant or pigment to each cup. Experiment with different color combinations to create interesting and captivating effects.

4. Resin Pour: Pour the different colors of resin onto your work surface randomly or in a specific pattern. Use a spatula, brush, or pipette to control the flow and distribution of colors.

5. Movements and Manipulations: Begin moving the resin on the surface using your hands or tools such as spatulas or brushes. Tilt the surface or gently blow on the resin to create unique movements and shapes.

6. Creating Effects: Explore various techniques like the "Flip Cup" (pouring into an upside-down cup and then inverting it), the "Swipe" (dragging an object along the resin to create streaks), or using a torch to generate air bubbles or smoke-like effects.

7.Drying and Finishing: Allow the resin to dry according to the manufacturer's instructions. Once fully dry, you can apply a protective coat of clear resin for a long-lasting, glossy finish.

2. THE ART OF INCLUSION: FIND OUT HOW TO ADD OBJECTS AND MATERIALS INSIDE THE RESIN

Using objects and materials within resin is a fascinating way to enrich your artwork and create visually interesting effects. The art of inclusion offers you the possibility to incorporate three-dimensional objects such as dried flowers, shells, beads, leaves, and any other element that can add a unique touch to your creation.

Preparation of Objects and Materials

Before you start working with resin, it's important to prepare the objects and materials you want to include. Ensure that the items are clean and free from dust or moisture. You can gently wash them with soap and water and dry them completely. If you're using organic items, such as flowers or leaves, make sure they're properly dried to avoid decay within the resin.

Placement of Objects in the Resin

Once the resin is ready to pour, you can place the objects within the mixture. You can arrange them in a specific design or drop them randomly for a more natural effect. Play with the arrangement of objects to create a sense of movement or depth within the resin.

Object Stabilization

To ensure that the objects remain in the desired position within the resin, you may need to use stabilizing techniques. You can do this with the help of wooden sticks, tweezers, or similar tools to hold the objects in place while the resin hardens. Make sure to place them inconspicuously or in a way that blends harmoniously with the artwork.

Experimenting with Different Objects and Materials

The art of inclusion offers endless creative possibilities. Don't limit yourself to just three-dimensional objects; also experiment with materials such as pigment powders, glitter, metallic leaves, or anything else that can add an interesting effect. You can embed these elements directly into the resin or gently sprinkle them on the surface for a more nuanced effect.

Luminous and Translucent Effects

The inclusion of objects and materials within the resin can create luminous and translucent effects, especially when using transparent or luminous elements. For example, including glass beads or small shards of mirror can reflect light and create a magical atmosphere in your artwork. You can also experiment with fluorescent or glow-in-the-dark pigments for glow-in-the-dark effects.

Level and Depth Design

The art of inclusion allows you to create layers and depths within the resin. You can place objects in a way that some are more in the foreground and others in the background, creating a sense of depth in your work. Play with the size and position of objects to achieve a captivating three-dimensional effect.

Versatility in the Choice of Objects

There are no limits to the choice of objects to include in the resin. You can use natural objects such as stones, shells, wood, or seeds, as well as artificial objects like buttons, beads, fabrics, or miniatures. Choose items that inspire you and fit the theme or concept you want to depict in your artwork.

Experimentation and Creativity

The art of inclusion is a field that offers ample room for experimentation and creativity. Don't be afraid to try new ideas and combinations of items. You can combine different materials, like resin and ceramic, to create an interesting contrast. Experiment with different arrangements and combinations of items to discover new effects and unique styles.

Be patient during the process of embedding objects in the resin, and be sure to follow the resin manufacturer's instructions for best results. Remember that constant practice and exploration will help you perfect your techniques and create truly unique works of art.

3. THE MAGIC OF CELL TECHNIQUE: CREATING OPEN AND CLOSED CELL EFFECTS FOR AN ORGANIC LOOK

The technique of using cells in resin is a fascinating method for creating organic and unique effects in your artwork. This technique simulates the appearance of cells, resulting in a vibrant, three-dimensional texture. You can achieve both open-cell effects, where cells are visible, and closed-cell effects, where cells are filled with color or translucent materials.

Preparation of Materials for Cell Effects

To create open or closed cell effects, you need to prepare the appropriate materials. You can use pigmented paints, glitter, mica powder, or other translucent materials to fill the cells. Prepare the materials in small quantities and ensure you have them on hand before you start pouring the resin.

Creating Open Cell Effects

To create open cell effects, pour a generous amount of clear resin onto the surface of your substrate. Then, using a thin object like a toothpick or skewer, gently make rolling motions across the surface to create the cells. Work delicately to avoid breaking any cells that form.

Creating Closed Cell Effects

Closed cell effects require an additional step of filling the cells with translucent or colored material. After creating the open cells as described above, carefully pour the selected material into the cells. You can use an eyedropper or a fine brush to control the flow of material and fill the cells evenly.

Experimentation and Creativity

The technique of using cells in resin offers a wide range of possibilities for experimentation and creativity. When working with this technique, you can play with a variety of colors and materials to create unique effects. Try combining different shades of translucent colors or mixing pigments to achieve interesting hues. You can also incorporate glitter, gold leaf, or other decorative elements to further enhance the appearance of your cells.

Control of Cell Flow and Density

To achieve an organic and natural look, it's important to control the flow and density of the cells.

You can adjust the amount of resin you pour and the way you create the rolling motions to achieve different cell sizes and shapes. Experiment with different techniques and take note of the results to develop your own distinctive style.

Finishing and Protecting the Cells

Once you have finished creating the cells and ensured that the resin is fully cured, it's important to focus on finishing and protecting your artwork. Follow these steps:

• Sanding: Use sandpaper of various grits to gently smooth the resin surface around the cells. This will help remove any bumps or protrusions, ensuring a smooth surface.

• Polishing: After smoothing, proceed to the polishing stage to enhance the shine of your cells. Use a resin-specific polishing compound and a soft cloth to gently buff the surface. This process will add luster and depth to your cells, making them visually appealing.

• Sealing: To protect your creations and preserve them over time, it is advisable to apply a layer of transparent sealant to the resin. This will help prevent yellowing and cracking of the resin over time. You can use a resin polish or a specific sealer recommended by the manufacturer.

• Storage: Once you have completed the finishing and protection of your cells, it is important to store them properly to safeguard them from dust, scratches, or damage. You can place your artworks in protective cases or display them in special arrangements to shield them from external influences.

4. PLAYS WITH CONTRAST: WORKING WITH COMPLEMENTARY COLORS AND BLENDING TECHNIQUES FOR DRAMATIC EFFECTS

Using complementary colors and blending techniques can transform resin into a medium of artistic expression full of contrasts, allowing you to create stunning and immersive visual effects.

Complementary Colors:

Using complementary colors in your resin artwork can create strong visual contrast and emotional impact.

Here are some examples of complementary colors:

• Blue and orange • Red and green • Purple and yellow

You can work with these complementary colors either by mixing them together or by using them in more subtle ways, such as in small shades or focal points within your composition.

Mixing Techniques:

Blending techniques allow you to create gradients and smooth transitions between colors. This adds depth and movement to your resin artwork. Here are some blending techniques you can explore:

• Marble: Pour different colors into the resin and use a stick or tool to create a marbled effect. You can make circular or linear movements to achieve different textures and patterns.

• Gradients: Pour two or more colors strategically, creating a gradient from one color to the next. You can use tilting techniques or apply successive layers to achieve smooth gradients and soft shades.

• Layers: Pour colors in successive layers, allowing them to partially overlap. This creates an effect of depth and transparency, allowing the colors to interact with each other in intriguing ways.

Experiments and Creativity:

Working with complementary colors and blending techniques offers endless creative possibilities. Experiment with different color combinations, variations in proportions, and application methods to achieve unique and surprising effects. Each attempt will lead you to discover new nuances and artistic possibilities.

Balance and Harmony:

As you experiment with complementary colors and blending techniques, keep in mind the importance of balance and harmony. Avoid letting the contrasts become too overpowering or chaotic. Strive for a balance between the colors, ensuring they blend harmoniously into your overall composition.

5. THE ART OF ACCIDENTALISM: EXPLOITING THE UNEXPECTED TO CREATE UNIQUE AND EXCITING WORKS

Accidental art is a creative technique that harnesses the power of unexpected and random results to create unique and exciting works of art with resin. This approach encourages artists to embrace mistakes and imperfections, transforming them into distinctive elements of their creations.

Here are some tips for making the most of the art of accidentalism in resin crafting:

Spontaneous Flow: Allow the resin to flow freely on your work surface without exerting too much control over the outcome. Experiment with different textures and viscosities of resin to achieve unexpected and interesting effects.

Chemical Reactions: Explore the chemical reactions between the resin and other materials. For example, you can add special pigments, dyes, or additives to the resin and observe how they interact with each other. These reactions can lead to surprising and unique effects.

Controlled Accidentalism: While accidentalism celebrates the unexpected, it is possible to have some degree of control over the process. For instance, you can strategically place objects or materials on your work surface before pouring the resin, allowing you to influence how the resin interacts with these elements.

Experimentation and Documentation: Experiment with different materials, colors, mixing techniques, and pouring methods to discover which combinations yield the desired effects. Throughout the process, keep a record of your experiments and the effects achieved. This will help you replicate and reproduce successful outcomes in the future.

Adaptation and Incorporation: If you encounter unexpected results or mistakes along the way, don't despair. Instead, try to adapt and incorporate these elements into your artwork. Often, the unexpected can add depth and interest to the final composition.

Finishing and Preservation: Once you have achieved the desired result, remember to apply a protective finish to your artwork to preserve it over time. This may involve applying a clear coat of resin or using specific paints and sealants.

CHAPTER 5 - LAYERS OF BEAUTY: CREATING ENCHANTING ART THROUGH THE ART OF LAYERING

1. DEPTH AND DIMENSION: UNLOCKING THE SECRETS OF LAYERING TO BRING YOUR WORKS TO LIFE

Layering is a captivating technique that allows you to create intriguing and three-dimensional works of art. By applying multiple layers of resin, each with its own unique characteristics, you can add depth, texture, and a sense of movement to your resin creations, bringing them to life.

One of the key secrets of layering lies in the careful selection of materials and objects to incorporate into each layer. You have a wide range of options, including color pigments, pearls, dried flowers, leaves, metallic threads, or any other objects you desire to incorporate into your artwork. These materials will infuse your creations with personality and originality, resulting in a unique and surprising visual effect.

To achieve maximum depth and dimension, it is important to plan the order of layers and the placement of objects within the resin carefully. By strategically positioning objects, playing with color and shape contrasts, and experimenting with different arrangements, you can create captivating visual effects. Remember that each layer contributes to a richer and more immersive three-dimensional experience.

During the layering process, patience and precision are crucial. Allow each layer to solidify properly before proceeding to the next, preventing unwanted blending or loss of detail. Techniques such as casting in thin layers or utilizing molds and masks can be employed to enhance the depth effects even further.

Color selection also plays a pivotal role in layering. You can experiment with bold combinations and color contrasts to achieve vibrant and eye-catching effects. Keep in mind that colors may slightly alter when immersed in resin, so it is advisable to conduct preliminary tests to evaluate the final effect before applying the entire layer.

2. THE POWER OF LAYERS: EXPERIMENTING WITH DIFFERENT LAYERING TECHNIQUES TO CREATE THREE-DIMENSIONAL EFFECTS

In addition to layering materials, there is a wide range of techniques that can be explored to achieve stunning three-dimensional effects.

Sequential Layering:

The sequential layering technique involves adding layers of resin one after another, allowing each layer to set before moving on to the next. This process ensures clear definition and separation between the layers. You can experiment with different color combinations and incorporate objects or materials between layers to create unique and layered effects.

Inclusion of Objects:

A creative way to add depth and dimension to your resin artwork is by including objects within the layers. Dried flowers, leaves, shells, stones, or any other interesting elements can be placed within the resin layer, ensuring they are completely covered. This creates a sense of depth and adds a tangible dimension to your creation.

Embossed Effects:

Take advantage of the ability to create relief effects using stencils or three-dimensional shapes. Place the desired stencil or object on the surface of your project and pour resin on top. Afterward, remove the stencil or object and allow the resin to cure. This will create an embossed effect that can be further enhanced by coloring or layering additional layers.

Brush Technique:

The brush technique involves using a brush or brushes to apply thin layers of resin to a surface. By utilizing brushes of different sizes and shapes, you can apply resin in a controlled manner, creating unique textures that add depth and movement to your work. This technique is particularly effective for creating effects such as waves, clouds, or gradients.

Layering with Pigments:

Using pigments during the layering process can yield amazing effects. Pigments can be mixed directly into the resin or applied between coats to create a colorful layering effect. Translucent or opaque pigments can be used to achieve the desired outcome.

Experiment with various color combinations and intensities to create a visually captivating depth and atmosphere in your artwork.

Depth Effects with Gradients:

Gradients are a fantastic technique for creating depth and visual layering effects. By using different colors of resin and gently pouring them onto the surface while lightly mixing with a stick or tool, you can achieve gradient effects. This technique produces a sense of depth and a smooth transition between layers, resulting in a visually captivating composition.

Incorporation of Three-Dimensional Elements:

For an even more dramatic three-dimensional effect, consider incorporating three-dimensional elements into your artwork. Beads, jewelry pieces, glass fragments, or any other objects with three-dimensional shapes and structures can be placed within the layers of resin. Take care to create a visually harmonious and balanced arrangement. This addition will introduce an element of drama and a tactile sense of depth to your artwork.

Thin Layer Processing:

An advanced layering technique involves applying thin layers of resin successively, allowing each layer to partially set before moving on to the next. This technique requires patience and precision but allows for the creation of highly detailed and intricate layering effects. By working in thin layers and adding details with brushes or precision tools, you can create landscapes or realistic images within your resin artwork.

3. PLAY WITH TRANSPARENCY: UTILIZING TRANSLUCENT MATERIALS TO CREATE LAYERS OF BEAUTY

The Use of Translucent Resins:

Translucent resins provide a unique opportunity to create layers of beauty with transparency effects. These materials allow partial light transmission, resulting in a captivating sense of depth and luminosity in your artwork.

Creating Glass Effects:

One of the most captivating applications of translucent resins is the ability to produce glass-like effects.

By pouring thin layers of translucent resin onto a prepared surface and allowing it to set, you can achieve a reflective glass effect that interacts suggestively with light. Experiment with different colors or incorporate translucent pigments for even more striking outcomes.

Layering Translucent Materials:

Another intriguing technique involves layering translucent materials within the resin. Embedding sheets of translucent plastic, delicate fabrics, or dried plant leaves within the resin layers creates a visually appealing layering effect where these materials overlap and generate depth. Ensure that you position translucent objects evenly and leave sufficient space between layers for the resin to allow light transmission.

Luminous Effects with Fluorescent Pigments:

To add a touch of enchantment and radiance to your artwork, consider using fluorescent pigments within translucent resin. These pigments react to UV light and emit a vibrant, intense glow. Incorporate the fluorescent pigments into the translucent resin and pour the layers onto your work surface. When exposed to UV light, the translucent resin layers infused with fluorescent pigments will illuminate, creating a spectacular and mesmerizing effect.

4. THE ART OF CONTROL: MASTERING THE LAYERING PROCESS FOR PRECISE AND ELEGANT RESULTS

Controlled Layering:

Layering is an art that demands control and precision. To achieve precise and elegant results, it is crucial to master the techniques of managing the layering process. This will enable you to control the position, quantity, and shape of each resin layer, allowing you to create the desired effects.

Planning and Preparation:

Prior to commencing the layering process, meticulous planning is essential. Consider the arrangement of layers, the desired colors, and the effects you wish to achieve. Prepare all necessary materials in advance, including measuring vessels, mixing utensils, and application tools.

Controlling Pour Times:

When layering, carefully monitor the pour times between layers.

Each subsequent layer should be poured once the previous layer has hardened sufficiently to support the weight of the next resin. This ensures distinct layers that remain separate and do not blend together.

Utilizing Physical Barriers:

To achieve clean lines and define specific areas within your artwork, employ physical barriers such as supports or separators during the pouring process. These barriers create boundaries between layers, enhancing precision.

Viscosity Control:

The viscosity of epoxy resin can impact control during layering. You can adjust the viscosity by incorporating resin-specific additives such as thinners. Thicker resin may be utilized for more pronounced effects, while a more fluid resin may be preferable for nuanced layering.

Experimentation and Practice:

Mastering control in layering requires experimentation and practice. Explore different pouring techniques, curing times, and the use of physical barriers. Document your results and learn from your experiments. This process will refine your skills and foster an intuition for the layering process.

Patience and Attention to Detail:

Layering demands patience and attention to detail. Take the time to perform each step with care and precision. Even minor details can significantly impact the final result of your artwork. Work in a calm environment, focus on the process, and relish the creative experience.

5. THE ALLURE OF MATTE LAYERS: UNLEASHING DRAMATIC EFFECTS WITH MATTE COVERAGE

Matte Coverage is a technique that enables the creation of dramatic effects using opaque layers of resin. This layering approach adds depth and mystery to your resin artwork, providing a striking contrast to sheer or glowing layers.

Matte Coverage Materials:

To achieve matte layers, you'll need materials specifically designed to produce this finish.

This may include opaque pigments, dyes, or additives tailored for epoxy resin. Ensure you utilize high-quality products that guarantee consistent results.

Application Techniques:

There are several techniques for applying opaque coverage. One of the most common methods involves mixing opaque pigments directly into the resin. Add the opaque pigment during the mixing stage and evenly distribute it within the desired layers. Other techniques may involve the use of matte sprays or specialty paints to create specific effects.

Thickness Control:

When applying the opaque cover, it is crucial to control the thickness of the layers. For a more intense effect, apply thicker layers of matte coverage. Conversely, for a subtler outcome, opt for thin, translucent layers. The objective is to achieve precise thickness control to create the desired effect.

Combined Effects:

Matte overlay can be used in combination with other effects, such as translucent or shimmer layers. Experiment with different materials and techniques to create unique and captivating combinations. You can also employ masks or masking tape to create precise shapes and boundaries between the opaque and transparent layers.

Creativity and Exploration:

Matte coverage offers endless creative possibilities. Be bold in exploring different combinations of colors, materials, and techniques. Experiment with various textures, blending effects, and intricate details. Let your creativity be inspired, allowing the matte layers to infuse drama into your resin artwork.

Practice and Refinement:

As with any artistic technique, practice is key to mastering the use of matte overlay. Experiment on small projects and take note of the results. Observe how matte coverage influences the overall appearance and ambiance of your artwork. Over time, you will develop the skill to precisely and creatively apply matte coverage.

CHAPTER 6 - THE ART OF INCLUSION: FROM NATURAL INCLUSIONS TO CUSTOMIZED CREATIONS

1. TREASURES OF NATURE: UTILIZING NATURAL MATERIALS TO CRAFT MAGICAL INCLUSIONS IN YOUR WORKS

Natural inclusions provide an extraordinary way to enhance your resin artwork. By incorporating materials from nature such as dried flowers, leaves, stones, and shells, you can create enchanting inclusions that capture the beauty and essence of the natural world. Explore different inclusion techniques and let your creativity soar, crafting one-of-a-kind works of art that evoke profound emotions.

The Beauty of Natural Inclusions

Natural inclusions embody the inherent beauty of nature. Each flower, leaf, or stone carries its own story and energy, and their incorporation into your artwork allows you to encapsulate a fragment of nature itself. Natural inclusions add an authentic and distinctive touch to your creations, providing a unique sensory experience for those who behold your works of art.

Selecting Natural Materials

When selecting natural materials for inclusions, the possibilities are endless. You can gather dried flowers and leaves during nature walks, collect shells along the seashore, or search for special stones in meaningful locations. Ensure that the materials you choose are compatible with the resin and can withstand the casting process. It is also important to properly prepare organic elements before incorporating them into the resin to ensure their durability.

Techniques for Including Natural Materials

There are various techniques for including natural materials in your resin artwork. You can delicately place them onto the resin layer before it fully hardens, creating a floating inclusion effect. Alternatively, you can immerse organic items in resin, ensuring they are fully covered and sealed to protect against moisture and decay. Additionally, you can create multiple layers with different inclusions, enhancing depth and dimension in your artwork.

Magic & Customized Achievements

Incorporating natural inclusions into your resin art grants you the ability to achieve magical and personalized results. Each inclusion contributes a sense of history and significance to your work, rendering it unique and irreplicable. You can create jewelry that showcases dried flowers, artwork that captures the beauty of seashells, or decorative pieces that encase special stones. Allow your creativity to shine through the selection and utilization of natural inclusions, crafting artworks that evoke emotions and forge deep connections with nature.

2. BEYOND THE ORDINARY: EXPERIMENT WITH UNCONVENTIONAL INCLUSIONS TO ADD A UNIQUE TOUCH TO YOUR CREATIONS

In resin art, your imagination knows no bounds. In addition to natural inclusions, there is a multitude of unconventional materials that can be used to create extraordinary effects and add a unique touch to your creations. Embrace the possibilities offered by unusual objects and unconventional materials, explore their potential, and let your creativity guide you. Don't be afraid to take risks and try new things, as it is through exploration that the doors to new forms of beauty and originality open.

Exploring New Creative Horizons

Unconventional inclusions present an opportunity to break free from the ordinary and venture into new creative horizons. You can incorporate found or recycled items, such as old buttons, fabric scraps, keys, beads, scrap metal, electronics, and even miniatures. These unconventional materials add an element of surprise and originality to your work, allowing you to create a unique and distinct aesthetic.

Experimentation and Discovery

Experimentation is key when working with unconventional inclusions. Try different combinations of unusual materials, observe their reactions with the resin, and explore how they interact with each other. You can create layers with various objects, experiment with layering techniques, and utilize advanced casting methods to achieve amazing effects. Remember that each unconventional inclusion carries its own unique potential, and you can only discover captivating combinations through experimentation.

Technical Considerations

When working with unconventional inclusions, it is important to consider a few technical aspects. Ensure that the materials you use are compatible with the resin and can withstand the casting process without suffering damage or undesired alterations. Properly prepare unusual objects before embedding them in resin by cleaning, sealing, or treating them to ensure their stability and durability.

Create Unique Works of Art

Experimenting with unconventional inclusions gives you the opportunity to create one-of-a-kind works of art that captivate attention and leave a lasting impression. Let your creativity run wild and fearlessly explore uncharted territories. Combine different materials, create intriguing contrasts, and seek inspiration wherever you go. Remember that resin art provides a platform for expressing yourself in a unique and personal way, and unconventional inclusions are a powerful tool for achieving that.

3. CUSTOMIZED INCLUSION: CREATE PERSONALIZED OBJECTS TO INCLUDE IN RESIN FOR A PERSONAL TOUCH

If you want to add a personal touch to your resin artwork, customized inclusion is the perfect way to do it. Creating personalized objects to include in resin allows you to add a unique and meaningful element to your creations, making them even more special. Customized inclusion is an exciting way to create resin artwork that reflects your creativity and personality.

Create Personalized Objects

Creating personalized objects to include in resin offers a unique opportunity to express your creativity and add a personal touch to your artwork. You can use a variety of materials such as polymer clay, colored resin, wood, stones, shells, fabric, paper, and more. Choose materials that inspire you and represent something meaningful to you, such as symbols, images, or personal memories.

Creation Techniques

There are several techniques you can use to create your customized inclusions. For example, you can shape objects using polymer clay and then bake them in the oven before embedding them in resin.

You can also create silicone molds to cast resin directly into and obtain custom three-dimensional objects. Other options include painting existing objects, creating mosaics or collages with fabric or paper, and using custom molds to cast resin into desired shapes.

Planning and Design

Before creating your customized inclusions, it is important to plan and design the desired end result. Take the time to define the concept and decide which materials and techniques will best suit your vision.

Technical Considerations

When working with customized inclusions, ensure that the materials you are using are compatible with the resin and can withstand the casting process without suffering damage or undesired alterations. Additionally, consider the size and shape of your inclusions in relation to the final artwork. Ensure they are small enough to be incorporated harmoniously into the resin, yet sturdy enough to withstand the test of time.

Create Personalized Artworks

Creating customized inclusions provides an opportunity to add a personal and meaningful touch to your resin artworks. Experiment with different techniques, materials, and designs to find the approach that best expresses your artistic vision. Remember that each customized inclusion you create carries a unique story and meaning, making your artworks even more special and personal.

4. THE ART OF BALANCE: DISCOVER HOW TO PLACE AND INCLUDE INCLUSIONS FOR A HARMONIOUS EFFECT

The Balance in the Composition

When working with inclusions in resin, achieving balance in the composition is essential for creating a harmonious effect. The art of balance involves strategically placing inclusions within your artwork to blend them seamlessly with the overall design. Here are some tips to help you achieve the perfect balance:

• Consider the size and shape of inclusions: Incorporate inclusions of various sizes and shapes to create visual contrast and movement in your composition.

Experiment with larger, more dramatic inclusions alongside smaller, more delicate ones for an interesting effect.

• Distribute inclusions evenly: Avoid clustering all the inclusions in one area of your artwork. Instead, distribute them evenly across the surface to create visual balance. You can create a pattern or layout with the inclusions for a more organized result.

• Embrace asymmetry: Balance in composition doesn't always require perfect symmetry. You can also achieve a balanced effect through asymmetry. Play with the arrangement of the inclusions to create a sense of movement and dynamism in your artwork.

• Create focal points: Use inclusions to create focal points within your composition. Place inclusions strategically to draw attention to specific areas or elements of your work. These focal points will help establish a sense of balance and guide the viewer's eye through your artwork.

The Harmonious Incorporation of Inclusions

In addition to placement, the harmonious incorporation of inclusions into your work is equally important. Here are some tips to ensure successful embedding:

• Immersion level: Choose the immersion level of the inclusions based on the desired effect. Some inclusions may be partially immersed in the resin for a subtle effect, while others may be fully immersed for better integration.

• Experiment with arrangements: Before permanently embedding the inclusions in the resin, try different arrangements. Place the inclusions on a flat surface to assess their appearance and placement before inserting them into your artwork.

• Layering: If you're working with inclusions of different sizes or types, create a layered effect by embedding them at different levels within the resin. This technique adds depth and dimension to your composition.

• Transparency and opacity: Inclusions can vary in transparency or opacity. Choose your inclusions carefully based on the desired visual effect. Transparent inclusions can create a sense of depth, while opaque inclusions add an element of mystery and contrast.

5. CARVED CREATIONS: USE CARVING TECHNIQUES TO ENGRAVE INCLUSIONS AND ADD PRECIOUS DETAILS

The Art of Carving

Carving is a captivating artistic technique that allows you to etch inclusions within the resin, adding intricate details and precious effects. It can be used to highlight specific elements or create unique patterns and designs. Here are some tips to help you make the most of carving techniques:

• Carving Tools: Utilize specialized carving tools such as chisels or metal points to carve inclusions into the resin. Ensure you have a variety of tools with different-sized tips to accommodate the various shapes and sizes of inclusions.

• Plan Your Design: Before you commence carving, carefully plan your design and determine which inclusions you want to emphasize or etch. You can create a preliminary sketch or test on a smaller resin piece to experiment with the design before working on the main artwork.

• Precise Engraving: Practice precision and work meticulously when carving. Employ gentle, controlled strokes to etch the inclusions, taking care not to damage the surrounding resin surface. Consider practicing carving on small test resin pieces to refine your technique before proceeding to the main work.

• Varying Depths: Explore different depths of carving to create captivating visual effects. Some inclusions can be carved more shallowly for a subtle effect, while others can be carved deeper for a more dramatic appearance. The variation in depths adds dimension and intrigue to your artwork.

Precious Details

In addition to carving inclusions, you can further enhance your creations with precious details. Here are some tips on how to incorporate these elements into your resin artwork:

• Embed Gems or Precious Stones: Delicately place small gems or precious stones within the resin to infuse your artwork with a touch of luxury and sparkle. Ensure they are securely fixed to prevent movement or shifting.

• Introduce Metallics: Utilize gold leaf, metal powder, or metallic threads to create metallic details within the resin. These elements can add elegance and sophistication to your creations.

• Utilize Paints and Pigments: Experiment with paints and pigments to introduce painted details or colorful effects within the resin. Employ fine brushes or precision tools to apply details with care.

• Work with Translucent Layers: Utilize translucent layers of resin to create captivating effects of depth and dimension. Apply thin layers of translucent resin to specific areas of your artwork to achieve glowing effects and gradients.

CHAPTER 7 - PROJECTS THAT INSPIRE: FROM JEWELRY TO HOME DECOR, CHOOSE YOUR STYLE

1. SPARKLING JEWELRY: CREATE UNIQUE PIECES TO EXPRESS YOUR PERSONALITY

Jewelry serves as a wonderful medium for expressing your unique personality. By working with resin, you can craft sparkling jewelry that captures attention and stands out. Here are some tips to help you create one-of-a-kind pieces:

• Selection of Materials: Opt for high-quality materials for your jewelry, such as chains, pendants, rings, or earrings. You can choose from precious metals like gold and silver, or explore alternative materials like stainless steel and brass. Ensure that the chosen materials are compatible with the resin.

• Luminous Inclusions: Leverage the translucent nature of resin to incorporate luminous inclusions in your jewelry. You can add bright pigments, glitters, or small gemstones to infuse your pieces with sparkle and radiance. Remember to strike the right balance with the inclusions for a harmonious appearance.

• Unique Shapes and Designs: Experiment with different shapes and designs to create truly distinctive jewelry. Utilize specialized resin molds to achieve intricate shapes or pour resin freely into open designs for a more organic and unrestrained aesthetic. Allow your creativity to flourish as you craft pieces that align with your personal style.

• Professional Finishing: Pay attention to the finishing touches of your jewelry to achieve a polished and enduring look. Utilize polishing techniques to create a smooth and lustrous surface. Additionally, consider applying a protective layer to the resin surface to preserve its appearance over time.

2. FUNCTIONAL ART OBJECTS: CREATE HOME DECORATIONS THAT BLEND AESTHETICS AND UTILITY

Home decorations can serve as true works of art, adding personality and style to your living spaces. By utilizing resin, you can create functional art objects that seamlessly combine aesthetics and utility. Here are some tips to get started:

• Selection of Base Objects: Choose base objects that are well-suited for resin, such as vases, coasters, trays, or photo frames. Ensure that the objects are clean and free from dust or residues that may affect the quality of your project.

• Themes and Styles: Determine the theme or style for your home decorations. You may opt for a natural look with dried flowers or leaves as inclusions, or you may prefer a more modern and abstract design using colored pigments and geometric shapes.

• Design Planning: Before beginning the project, plan the design of your functional art object. Consider the arrangement of inclusions, color choices, and distribution of elements within the resin. You can sketch or create a draft to help visualize the final result.

• Preparation of Base Objects: Prepare the base objects by thoroughly cleaning them and ensuring they are ready for resin application. If necessary, protect areas that you do not want to be covered with resin using adhesive tape or other protective materials.

• Pouring the Resin: Pour the resin into the base objects following the manufacturer's instructions. Ensure that you mix the resin well to avoid air bubbles. You can add pigments, glitters, or other inclusions of your choice to personalize your project.

• Placement of Inclusions: Position the inclusions within the resin according to your planned design. You can use tweezers or a toothpick to place the inclusions precisely and accurately.

• Removal of Air Bubbles: Use a toothpick or stirrer to remove any trapped air bubbles in the resin. Gently run the toothpick over the resin surface to coax the bubbles upward.

• Resin Curing: Allow the resin to cure following the recommended drying times provided by the manufacturer. Ensure that the objects are placed on a flat and leveled surface during the curing process to prevent the resin from shifting.

• Finishing and Polishing: Once the resin has completely cured, remove the objects from molds or work surfaces. If necessary, perform light sanding to remove any imperfections or protrusions. Subsequently, you can polish the resin surface using a resin-specific polishing agent.

• Utilizing the Functional Art Object: Now that you have completed your project, you can use the functional art object to enhance your home. You can display it on a table as a decorative element or utilize it for a specific function, such as a coaster or a flower vase.

3. LIGHT AND COLOR: EXPERIMENT WITH BUILT-IN LIGHTS AND PIGMENTS TO CREATE STUNNING EFFECTS

Light and color are essential elements in creating extraordinary works of art with epoxy resin. By incorporating lights and pigments into your creations, you can add a touch of magic and charm.

Here are some techniques to explore:

Illuminate Your World: Using Built-in LED Lights

LED lights have the power to completely transform the appearance and ambiance of your resin artwork. Follow these steps to incorporate LED lights into your designs:

1. Select the type of LED light you want to use, such as LED strip lights, individual LED lights, or battery-operated lights.

2. Prepare the base of your resin creation, ensuring that it has empty spaces or channels for placing the lights.

3. Position the LED lights as desired, aiming to distribute them evenly and accentuate the most interesting parts of your work.

4. Securely affix the LED lights in the resin using transparent glue or epoxy resin to prevent them from shifting.

5. Connect the LED lights to a suitable power source and turn them on to witness the luminous effect they create on your resin creation.

Play with Pigments: Add Color and Depth

Pigments are versatile tools for adding vibrant color and depth to your resin creations. Here are some tips for experimenting with pigments:

1. Choose the pigments you want to use, such as powdered or liquid pigments, and select a variety of colors that suit your project.

2. Prepare your epoxy resin according to the manufacturer's instructions and add the desired pigments. You can mix different pigments together to create new shades or achieve subtle variations.

3. Pour the colored resin into your chosen mold or shape, ensuring even distribution.

4. Use a mixing stick or a similar tool to create marbled effects or gradients within the resin.

5. If you desire more complex effects, consider embedding multiple layers of colored resin, allowing each layer to partially set before pouring the next.

6. Allow the resin to fully cure following the manufacturer's instructions and admire the stunning effects created by the pigments in your resin project.

4. CUSTOMIZE YOUR ENVIRONMENT: IDEAS AND TIPS TO ADAPT PROJECTS TO YOUR NEEDS

Everyone has different tastes and styles when it comes to decorating their living space. Here are some ideas and tips on how to personalize resin projects to adapt them to your needs and unique style.

Discover Your Style: Identify Your Personal Taste

Before diving into customizing projects, it's important to identify your personal style. Consider what colors, themes, or decorative elements attract you the most. Here are some suggestions to help you discover your style:

• Gather inspiration from magazines, websites, social media, or existing artworks.

• Create a mood board or image album that reflects your tastes and preferences.

• Take note of colors, shapes, and themes that frequently appear in your choices.

Once you have identified your style, you will be able to personalize resin projects to suit your environment.

Choose Materials and Colors that Blend with Your Decor

When customizing resin projects, consider the existing decor in your home or the space where you plan to display the artworks. Choose materials and colors that blend harmoniously with your decor to create a cohesive effect. For example:

• If your decor is dominated by neutral tones, you might opt for subtle and delicate colors in your resin creations.

• If you have a modern and minimalist decor, you might choose clean and linear shapes for your resin projects.

Personalize the Details: Add Meaningful Elements

To make resin projects even more personal, consider adding meaningful elements. Here are some ideas:

• Include objects or materials that hold emotional value for you, such as a seashell collected during a vacation or a piece of fabric that is significant to you.

• Add initials or words that represent important values or concepts in your life.

• Experiment with textures or patterns that evoke your passions or interests, such as nature, art, or music.

CHAPTER 8 - OVERCOMING THE OBSTACLES: TIPS AND SOLUTIONS TO AVOID COMMON RESIN PROCESSING PROBLEMS

1. DEFEAT AIR BUBBLES: TECHNIQUES FOR ACHIEVING A SMOOTH AND FLAWLESS SURFACE

Working with resin can be a rewarding experience, but it can also present some challenges to overcome, such as the formation of air bubbles in the resin. These bubbles can mar the final appearance of your project. Learn different techniques to defeat air bubbles and achieve a smooth and flawless surface. Follow these tips for the best results:

Material Preparation

One common cause of air bubbles is improper material preparation. Here are some guidelines for preparing resin properly:

• Carefully mix the epoxy following the manufacturer's instructions. Ensure that the components are thoroughly and accurately mixed to prevent the formation of air bubbles during the curing process.

• Allow the mixture to rest for a few minutes before starting to pour, allowing any air bubbles to rise to the surface and disappear.

Use of a Torch or Flame

An effective way to remove air bubbles is to use a torch or flame to heat the resin surface. Here's how you can proceed:

• After pouring the resin, gently pass a torch or flame over the surface. This will help break up any smaller air bubbles and cause them to rise to the surface.

• Make sure to keep the torch or flame at a safe distance to avoid damage or overheating of the resin.

Using a Vacuum Chamber

A professional option for eliminating air bubbles is to use a vacuum chamber. This device creates a vacuum that efficiently extracts air bubbles from the resin. Here's how to use it:

• Pour the resin into the vacuum chamber and start the device.

• The vacuum agitation will cause air bubbles to rise to the surface, allowing you to easily remove them.

Using a Bubble Removal Tool

You can also use a specialized tool to remove air bubbles while pouring the resin. Here are some useful tools:

• Fine bristle brush: Gently brush the surface of the resin to break up any air bubbles.

• Needle or toothpick: Use a needle or toothpick to puncture and break up any larger air bubbles that rise to the surface.

Always remember to use these tools gently to avoid damaging the resin surface.

Cover and Rest

After working with the resin, cover your project with a lid or dome to protect it from dust and debris that could cause air bubbles to form. Allow the resin to rest in a disturbance-free environment, allowing any air bubbles to emerge and disappear.

2. ACHIEVING A FLAWLESS TRANSPARENT RESIN: PREVENTING STAINS AND UNDESIRABLE RESIDUE

When working with clear resin, it is crucial to create a pristine surface that is free from unwanted stains or residue. Below, you will discover techniques that will help you avoid the appearance of stains and achieve a perfect transparent finish. Follow these tips for optimal results:

Cleaning and Preparation

Properly cleaning and preparing the surfaces is essential to prevent the occurrence of unwanted stains or residues. Before starting the resin-working process, ensure that the surfaces are clean, dry, and free from dust or debris. Thoroughly clean the surfaces using a clean, lint-free cloth to remove any dirt or grease.

Leveling and Smoothing

Leveling and sanding the surfaces are vital steps to achieve a smooth and even finish. When pouring the resin, distribute it evenly over the surface of your project.

Utilize a leveling tool, such as a putty knife or wooden dowel, to spread the resin evenly and remove any excess. After pouring, carefully inspect the surface and use a tool to smooth out any bumps or air bubbles.

Adequate Coverage

Properly covering your project during the resin curing process is crucial to prevent the appearance of stains or dust. Here's what you can do:

• Use a lid or dome to cover your project and protect it from dust, hair, or other debris that may fall onto the resin as it cures.

• If you notice any dust or debris on the surface while the resin is curing, gently remove it using a tool such as a fine-bristled toothbrush.

Post-Treatment

Once the resin has fully cured, you may encounter unwanted stains or residue. Here are some solutions you can try:

• Use a specific cleaning solution designed for clear resin and gently wipe the surface to remove any stains or residue.

• If the stains persist, you can try gently sanding the surface with fine grit sandpaper. Proceed with caution to avoid damaging the resin.

3. TIME AND TEMPERATURE: PRECISE MANAGEMENT OF VARIABLES FOR OPTIMAL RESULTS

When working with resin, precise control of time and temperature is crucial for achieving the best outcomes. Follow these tips to ensure accurate time and temperature management:

Mixing Time

Properly mixing the resin components is essential for thorough curing and optimal results.

• Adhere to the manufacturer's instructions regarding the recommended mixing time. Typically, stirring for 2-3 minutes is recommended to ensure thorough blending.

• Use an effective mixing tool, such as a wooden stick or spatula, to ensure even distribution of the components.

Working Time

Working time refers to the duration during which the resin remains in a liquid and workable state. Understanding this period is crucial for executing desired techniques. Consider the following:

• Familiarize yourself with the specific working time of the resin product you are using, as it can vary based on resin type and brand.

• Factor in the working time when employing techniques like layering, embedding objects, or applying pigments. Ensure that these operations are completed within the working time before the resin starts to cure.

Ambient Temperature

The ambient temperature can impact the resin's hardening and workability. Follow these guidelines to manage temperature effectively:

• Adhere to the manufacturer's recommendations regarding the recommended ambient temperature when working with resin.

• Avoid working in excessively cold or hot environments, as it can affect the resin's chemical reaction and curing process.

• If necessary, adjust the room temperature using tools such as heaters or air conditioners to maintain a stable environment.

Curing Time

Curing time refers to the period during which the resin solidifies and fully cures. Respecting this time frame is crucial for ensuring the strength and durability of your creations. Consider the following:

• Consult the manufacturer's instructions for the recommended curing time, which can vary based on the resin type and formulation.

• Refrain from touching or handling your creations during the curing period to prevent damage or deformation.

• Take into account the ambient temperature during curing, as lower temperatures may impact the curing speed.

4. THE STICKY PROBLEM: STRATEGIES TO ADDRESS NATURAL RESIN ADHESION

Resin, due to its nature, can often become sticky and attract dust and debris. However, there are strategies you can employ to tackle this stickiness issue and keep your resin creations clean and appealing.

Apply a Sealant

Using a sealant on the resin surface is an effective method to reduce tackiness and safeguard your creations. You can opt for a clear spray sealant or a clear gel. It is important to carefully follow the manufacturer's instructions for proper application and drying time.

Clean with Isopropyl Alcohol

Isopropyl alcohol serves as an effective solvent for eliminating stickiness from resin. Dampen a cotton cloth with isopropyl alcohol and gently rub the sticky surface. Ensure that you use high-quality isopropyl alcohol and test its effect on a small inconspicuous area of your creation before applying it more broadly.

Talcum Powder

Talcum powder can help reduce the stickiness of resin. Lightly dust a small amount of talcum powder on the sticky surface and gently rub it with a soft cloth. Be diligent in removing any excess talcum powder to avoid affecting the appearance of your creation.

Proper Storage

Appropriate storage of your resin creations can minimize stickiness. Consider the following tips:

• Store your creations in a cool, dry place away from direct sunlight or heat sources.

• Utilize sealed cases or containers to shield your creations from dust and external elements.

• Avoid stacking your resin creations, as this may cause surfaces to adhere to one another.

5. CREATIVE RESCUE: SOLUTIONS TO CORRECT MISTAKES AND TURN THEM INTO OPPORTUNITIES

Resin crafting is a creative and thrilling process, but occasionally mistakes or unexpected mishaps can occur. However, don't despair! There are creative solutions that will enable you to rectify mistakes and transform them into opportunities to create unique works of art. Consider the following solutions:

Repairing Cracks or Fissures

If your resin creation develops cracks or fissures, you can utilize a clear epoxy adhesive to repair them. Apply the adhesive along the crack or crevice and join the parts together. It is important to meticulously follow the manufacturer's instructions regarding drying time and final strength of the adhesive.

Concealing Imperfections with Decorative Materials

Should you encounter any imperfections or blemishes on the surface of your creation, you can camouflage them by incorporating decorative materials such as glitter, sequins, beads, or small objects. Apply a thin layer of clear resin to the surface and creatively arrange the decorative materials to conceal the imperfections. Allow the resin to cure as instructed by the manufacturer.

Transforming Mistakes into Design Elements

Mistakes can be transformed into distinctive design elements. For instance, if you encounter air bubbles in your creation, instead of viewing them as flaws, you can integrate them into the design and highlight them as unique features. You can even create "troubled water" or "cloud" effects surrounding the air bubbles to make your creation even more captivating.

Adding Details and Enhancements

If a specific part of your resin creation does not meet your expectations, you can enhance its appearance by incorporating additional details or accentuating certain elements. Acrylic paint, fine brushes, or other materials can be used to add intricate details, texture, or lighting effects. Remember to allow any added materials to fully dry before applying a clear sealer.

CHAPTER 9 - EXPLORING NEW HORIZONS: INSPIRATION FROM SUCCESSFUL ARTISTS AND INNOVATIVE TRENDS

1. VISIONARIES OF RESIN ART: STORIES OF ARTISTS WHO REVOLUTIONIZED THE USE OF EPOXY RESIN

In the realm of epoxy resin art, there have been artists who have pushed boundaries and revolutionized the utilization of this versatile material. These visionaries have elevated resin art to unprecedented levels, pioneering innovative techniques and creating extraordinary masterpieces. Here are a few tales of artists who have left a significant mark in the field:

Bruce Riley

Bruce Riley is an American artist renowned for his abstract works crafted with epoxy resin. His creations are characterized by a fusion of vibrant colors, organic shapes, and captivating textures. Riley experiments with various layering and color-mixing techniques to produce artwork that exudes fluidity and vitality. His mastery in controlling the resin's flow and harmoniously incorporating materials has earned him great acclaim in the contemporary art world.

Miha Brinovec

Miha Brinovec is a celebrated Slovenian artist specializing in the use of epoxy resin to forge artworks that blend sculpture and painting. His pieces feature human and animal figures in motion, crafted with extraordinary attention to detail and a sense of weightlessness. Brinovec employs resin to create three-dimensional and translucent effects, skillfully playing with light and shadows to breathe life into his creations. His unique approach to resin art has captivated art enthusiasts worldwide.

Riusuke Fukahori

Riusuke Fukahori is a Japanese artist renowned for his resin works that flawlessly replicate fish and other aquatic creatures in astonishingly realistic fashion. Fukahori employs an innovative technique called "fish painting," in which he meticulously paints layers of transparent resin to create the illusion of fish and submerged objects within an aquatic environment.

His pieces seamlessly merge painting and sculpture, demanding precision and patience. Fukahori's meticulous and lifelike approach has garnered significant acclaim and international recognition.

Laura Moriarty

Laura Moriarty is an American artist who has expanded the horizons of epoxy resin art by exploring the interconnectedness of art, science, and nature. Her portfolio encompasses sculptures and environmental installations that utilize resin to fashion organic shapes and fantastical landscapes. Moriarty draws inspiration from natural formations, such as rocks and minerals, employing resin to recreate their distinct qualities and textures. Her works evoke a sense of wonder, inviting contemplation on our relationship with nature and the world around us.

2. ADVANCED EXPERIMENTS: EXPERIMENTAL AND INNOVATIVE TECHNIQUES TO TAKE YOUR ART TO A NEW LEVEL

In the realm of resin art, delving into experimental and innovative techniques can elevate your creative endeavors to unprecedented heights. Here are some advanced techniques that can help you create unique and awe-inspiring art with epoxy resin.

Smoke and Fog Effects

One intriguing technique to explore is the creation of smoke and fog effects within your resin works. You can achieve this by using translucent or diluted opaque pigments to produce a subtle and ethereal smoke-like appearance that gracefully meanders through the resin. This imparts a sense of mystique and depth, adding an extra dimension to your creations.

Incorporation of Three-Dimensional Materials

Beyond incorporating flat or thin inclusions, you can experiment with integrating three-dimensional materials into your resin works. For instance, you can embed small objects such as dried flowers, gems, miniatures, or shards of glass within the resin layer to achieve captivating depth and intricate detailing effects. This technique imbues your creations with a tactile and visual allure.

Utilization of Colored and Transparent Resins

To create captivating color effects, consider working with colored and transparent resins in conjunction.

Layering different colors of resin allows you to achieve unique gradient and transparency effects, opening up a vast realm of possibilities for crafting dynamic and mesmerizing works of art.

Suspension Technique

The suspension technique enables you to create artworks that appear to float within the resin medium. By suspending objects such as stones, crystals, beads, or even small sculptures within the resin layer, you infuse your creations with a captivating sense of movement and depth, resulting in visually striking and engaging effects.

Iridescent and Metallic Effects

Incorporating iridescent or metallic pigments into your resin artwork can impart a magical and luminous appearance. These pigments produce a color-changing effect depending on the viewing angle, bestowing your creation with a dynamic and enchanting allure. Experimenting with iridescent pigments, such as mother-of-pearl black or iridescent azure, can yield stunning light and reflection effects.

Sustainability and Ecological Materials

Increasingly, artists are embracing sustainability and environmentally friendly practices in resin art. There is a growing interest in utilizing eco-friendly and sustainable materials for resin production. Exploring alternatives such as water-based resins or recycled resins allows artists to reduce their environmental impact while upholding their commitment to responsible artistry.

3. BEYOND THE RESIN: COMBINED MATERIALS AND MIXED TECHNIQUES TO CREATE ECLECTIC AND UNIQUE WORKS

Taking your artwork to new heights involves exploring the integration of resin with various mixed materials and media, resulting in eclectic and one-of-a-kind masterpieces.

Incorporation of Fabrics and Textile Materials

Enhance your resin creations by incorporating fabrics or textile materials. Embedding pieces of fabric, lace, thread, or rope within the resin layer adds texture and a tactile dimension to your artwork. This juxtaposition of materials creates a captivating contrast and enhances the visual depth of your creation.

Carving on Solid Materials

Utilize the carving technique to add intricate detail and texture to solid materials combined with resin. Carve patterns or designs on wood, metal, stone, or other materials, and then fill the carved recesses with colored resin to accentuate the intricacies. This technique showcases skilled craftsmanship and creates a striking contrast between the resin and solid material.

Paint and Resin

The fusion of paint and resin can yield extraordinary artworks. Paint an image onto a surface, such as a canvas or wood panel, and then overlay it with a layer of clear resin to achieve depth and sheen. This technique infuses your creation with a sense of realism and vitality.

Collage and Resin

Merge the realms of collage and resin for captivating mixed-media creations. Assemble a collage using diverse materials like paper, photographs, fabrics, or three-dimensional objects, and seal it with a transparent resin layer. This amalgamation of elements results in a distinctive composition and offers limitless creative possibilities.

Incorporation of Natural Elements

Combine resin with natural elements, such as stones, shells, leaves, or dried flowers, to craft nature-inspired artwork. These elements can be embedded within the resin layer or placed on the surface of your creation. This amalgamation of natural elements and resin evokes a sense of wonder and yields unique and evocative works of art.

CHAPTER 10 - KEEPING EXCELLENCE: GUIDE TO THE CARE AND CONSERVATION OF RESIN WORKS

1. MAINTAINING BEAUTY OVER TIME: TIPS FOR CLEANING, MAINTENANCE, AND PROTECTION OF RESIN WORKS

Resin works are incredibly beautiful and captivating, but it is crucial to care for them to preserve their allure over time. Follow these practical tips for proper cleaning, maintenance, and protection to safeguard the shine and integrity of your resin creations.

Regular Cleaning

Regular cleaning is essential to keep your resin works clean and free from accumulated dust or dirt. Use a soft, slightly damp cloth to gently clean the resin surface. Avoid harsh or abrasive cleaners that can damage the protective coating of the resin.

Handle with Care

Treat your resin works with delicacy and caution to avoid accidental scratching or bumping. When moving or cleaning them, ensure proper support and avoid sudden movements that could cause damage. Remember that resin can be fragile, so handling it carefully will help preserve its integrity over time.

Stain Treatment

If you notice any stains on the resin surface, gently treat them with a soft cloth dipped in warm water and neutral soap. Avoid using solvents or harsh chemicals that could harm the resin. If the stain persists, consult a professional for further advice.

Proper Storage

When storing your resin artwork for an extended period, ensure it is done correctly to prevent damage or deformation. Store them in cool, dry environments away from direct sunlight. Protect them with covers or specialized cases to shield against dust, moisture, or accidental impact.

Use of Protective Coatings

Applying a protective coating to the resin surface can help safeguard it from wear. Various coating options are available, such as clear coats or protective resins specifically formulated for resin works. Follow the manufacturer's instructions and apply the coating in a well-ventilated area. This creates a protective layer that preserves shine and reduces wear and tear over time.

Avoid Harmful Substances

Prevent exposure of resin works to harsh chemicals or liquids that can damage them. For instance, avoid cleaning products containing ammonia, alcohol, or thinners, as they can dull or stain the resin surface. Also, refrain from placing hot objects directly on the resin, as they may cause irreversible damage.

Periodic Maintenance

Perform periodic maintenance on your resin works to ensure their good condition over time. Regularly inspect the surface for signs of wear, stains, or damage. If any issues are detected, take immediate action to address them.

2. PERFECT EXPOSURE: TIPS FOR POSITIONING AND LIGHTING RESIN WORKS

Proper positioning and lighting are crucial for showcasing the beauty and visual impact of resin works. Follow these tips and guidelines to enhance the presentation of your resin artwork.

Choice of Location

Select the display location for your resin works thoughtfully. Consider the surroundings, natural lighting, and decor of the space. Look for a position that highlights your artwork and blends harmoniously with the environment. Avoid areas exposed to direct sunlight, as it may cause fading or deterioration of the resin over time.

Adequate Lighting

Lighting is paramount in showcasing resin works. Use a combination of natural and artificial light sources to bring out the details and effects of the resin. Avoid fluorescent or bright lights, as they can alter the colors and appearance of the artwork. Experiment with different light positions to achieve the desired effect.

Supports and Bases

Utilize suitable stands or bases to display your resin works. Ensure that the stand is stable and secure, preventing falls or damage to the artwork. You can opt for clear or neutral stands to accentuate the levitating effect or choose bases that complement the theme or style of the artwork.

UV Protection

Sunlight and UV rays can damage resin over time. If you intend to display your resin works in bright environments or areas exposed to direct sunlight, consider using anti-reflective glass or protective films to reduce UV exposure. This will help preserve the colors and durability of the artwork.

Periodic Rotation

To prevent wear and extended exposure to specific areas of your resin artwork, periodically rotate the pieces. By repositioning the exhibits, you can distribute wear evenly and maintain a uniform appearance over time.

3. REPAIR AND RESTORATION: STRATEGIES TO ADDRESS ANY DAMAGE OR DEFECTS OVER TIME

Despite the care and attention given to resin works, it's possible for damage or defects to occur over time. Here are some strategies and tips to address any problems and restore your resin works.

Assessment of Damages

Before attempting any repair or restoration, thoroughly assess the type and extent of damage to your resin work. This evaluation will help determine the best approach and prevent unnecessary or harmful interventions.

Repairing Cracks and Minor Defects

For cracks or minor flaws in the resin, you can use clear resin to fill and repair the damaged area. Ensure that you clean the area thoroughly, carefully apply the resin, and level the surface using an appropriate tool. Allow the resin to dry and harden completely before proceeding with further steps.

Restoring Color and Luster

If the resin work has lost its color or shine over time, there are several strategies to restore its original appearance. You can use pigments or sheer dyes to revive faded colors. Additionally, gentle polishing with specific products can help restore the original shine.

Repairing Structural Damages

In the case of significant structural damage, such as broken parts or loss of detail, a more complex intervention may be required. You might need to utilize specific resins, adhesives, or modeling techniques to repair or rebuild the damaged area. It's advisable to seek the assistance of an expert or skilled craftsman to ensure high-quality and precise repairs.

Prevention and Conservation

The best strategy to address damage or defects in resin works is to prevent such issues through proper conservation and care. Avoid exposing the works to extreme temperatures, humidity, and direct sunlight. Handle your resin artworks with care and provide adequate protection during transport or storage.

CHAPTER 11 - PROJECT IDEAS: START CREATING YOUR FIRST EPOXY RESIN OBJECTS

PROJECT 1: LAMP WITH INCORPORATED LED LIGHTS

Get ready to create your own unique resin lamp with incorporated LED lights. Follow the step-by-step instructions below to bring your project to life.

Necessary materials:

• Transparent epoxy resin

• Epoxy resin hardener

• Lamp molds (available online or at craft stores in various types)

• LED lights (battery or adapter powered)

• Resin-based colors (optional)

• Glitter or other decorative elements (optional)

• Latex gloves

• Mixing rods

• Trowel or other tool for removing air bubbles

• Scotch tape

• Scissors

• Drill (optional)

Step-by-step instructions:

1. Put on latex gloves to protect your hands during the resin handling process.

2. Carefully follow the manufacturer's instructions to prepare the epoxy resin by mixing the resin and hardener in the correct ratio.

3. If desired, add resin-based paints to introduce color into the resin. Mix a few drops of paint into the resin mixture thoroughly.

4. For an extra touch, mix glitter or other decorative elements into the resin, ensuring they are well distributed.

5. Prepare the lamp mold and place the LED lights inside. Ensure that the

6. Pour the prepared epoxy resin into the mold, ensuring that the LED lights are completely covered and leaving enough space for the lamp base.

7. If you wish to create a layered effect or incorporate decorative elements, allow the first layer of resin to harden slightly before pouring additional layers.

8. Use a trowel or scraper tool to gently remove any air bubbles that may have formed on the resin surface. You can lightly tap the surface or use a wooden stick to pop the bubbles.

9. Cover the mold with scotch tape to prevent dust or other debris from settling on the resin surface as it cures.

10. Allow the resin to cure in the mold for the recommended time specified by the manufacturer's instructions. This typically takes several hours or longer, depending on the type of resin used.

11. If desired, once the resin has hardened slightly, you can use a drill to create a hole for the LED light wire to pass through.

12. Carefully remove the lamp from the mold once the resin has fully cured.

13. Use scissors to trim any excess resin around the lamp to achieve your desired shape.

14. Cut the LED light wire to an appropriate length for connecting to a power source or battery.

15. Connect the LED lights' cable to a power source or battery and turn on the lights to see the glowing effect of your resin lamp.

PROJECT 2: COLORED EARRINGS

Get ready to create beautiful colored epoxy resin earrings. Follow the step-by-step instructions to make this unique accessory.

Necessary materials:

• Transparent epoxy resin

• Resin-based colors (liquid pigments or mica powders)

• Earring molds (preferably silicone)

• Plastic or wooden mixing sticks

• Measuring cups (graduated)

• Protective gloves

• Fine grit sandpaper

• Earring hooks

• Connecting rings

• Jewelry pliers

Step-by-step instructions:

1. Protect your work surface with a plastic sheet or protective mat.

2. Make sure you work in a well-ventilated area. Wear protective gloves.

3. Measure out the required amount of clear epoxy according to the manufacturer's instructions.

4. Use the graduated measuring cups to ensure the right ratio of epoxy to hardener.

5. Pour the epoxy into a clean container.

6. Add resin-based colors (liquid pigments or mica powders) according to your preferences.

7. Mix thoroughly with a mixing stick until you get a uniform color.

8. Prepare the earring molds by placing them on a flat and stable surface.

9. Carefully pour the colored resin into the molds, filling them to the brim.

10. Make sure there are no trapped air bubbles. You can use a gas torch or air bubble stirrer to remove air bubbles.

Gently pass the flame of the torch over the surface of the resin to bring out the bubbles. If you prefer, you can use an air bubble shaker to manually remove them.

11. Leave the resins in the molds in a dust-free area away from drafts. Follow the manufacturer's instructions for the required curing time.

12. Once the resin has fully cured, carefully remove the earrings from the molds. You can bend the molds slightly to make it easier to remove.

13. Use fine grit sandpaper to smooth out any bumps or ridges on the edges of the earrings. You can polish the surface with a soft cloth or resin polisher if you want a shinier look.

14. Using the jewelry pliers, attach the connecting rings to the earrings.

15. Connect the earring hooks to the connecting rings.

PROJECT 3: FLORAL RING

Get ready to create a stunning epoxy resin floral ring. Follow the step-by-step instructions to make this unique piece of jewelry.

Necessary materials:

- Transparent epoxy resin
- Hardener for epoxy resin
- Ring molds (various types available online or at craft stores)
- Resin-based colors (optional)
- Glitter or other decorative elements (optional)
- Latex gloves
- Mixing rods
- Trowel (or other tool) for removing air bubbles
- Scissors

Step-by-step instructions:

1. Wear latex gloves to protect your hands when using the resin. Prepare the epoxy following the manufacturer's instructions carefully, mixing the resin and hardener in the correct ratio.

2. If you want to add color to the resin, you can do so using resin-based paints. Add a few drops to the mixture and mix well.

3. You can also spice up the look of the ring by adding glitter or other decorative elements. Mix the elements in the resin carefully.

4. Pour the prepared epoxy resin into your ring mold. Make sure you don't fill the mold completely, leaving enough space for any inclusions or additional layers.

5. If you want to create a layered effect, allow the resin to harden slightly for a few minutes and then pour another color or layer of resin on top.

6. Use a trowel or scraper tool to gently remove any air bubbles that form on the resin surface.

You can tap the surface gently or use a wooden stick to pop the bubbles.

7. If you want to add decorative elements such as dried flowers or leaves, place them gently on the resin surface. Press them lightly to make them adhere.

8. Leave the ring in the mold for the curing time indicated by the resin manufacturer's instructions. Usually, this will take several hours or more depending on the type of resin used.

9. Once the resin has fully cured, carefully remove the ring from the mold.

10. Use scissors to trim any excess resin around the ring to achieve the desired shape.

PROJECT 4: COASTERS

Get ready to create beautiful resin coasters to add a touch of elegance to your home decor. Follow these step-by-step instructions to make your own unique set of coasters.

Necessary materials:

• Transparent epoxy resin

• Hardener for epoxy resin

• Coaster molds (various types available online or at craft stores)

• Resin-based colors (optional)

• Glitter or other decorative elements (optional)

• Latex gloves

• Mixing rods

• Trowel (or other tool) for removing air bubbles

• Scotch tape

• Fine grit sandpaper

• Clear spray paint (optional)

Step-by-step instructions:

1. Wear latex gloves to protect your hands when using the resin. Prepare the epoxy following the manufacturer's instructions carefully, mixing the resin and hardener in the correct ratio.

2. If you want to add color to the resin, you can do so using resin-based paints. Add a few drops to the mixture and mix well.

3. You can also spice up the look of the coasters by adding glitter or other decorative elements. Mix the elements in the resin carefully.

4. Prepare the coaster molds, making sure they are clean and dry.

5. Pour the prepared epoxy into the molds, filling them to the brim or to the desired amount.

6. If you want to create a layered effect or include decorative elements, you can pour additional layers of resin after allowing the first layer to harden slightly.

7. Use a trowel or scraper tool to gently remove any air bubbles that form on the resin surface. You can tap the surface gently or use a wooden stick to pop the bubbles.

8. Cover the molds with scotch tape to prevent dust or other debris from settling on the surface of the resin as it cures.

9. Allow the resin to cure in the molds for the curing time indicated by the manufacturer's instructions. Usually, this will take several hours or more depending on the type of resin used.

10. Once the resin has fully cured, carefully remove the coasters from the molds.

11. Use fine-grit sandpaper to smooth out any bumps or irregularities on the surface of the coasters.

12. If you want a glossy, protective finish, you can apply a coat of clear spray paint to the surface of the coasters. Follow the manufacturer's instructions for proper application.

PROJECT 5: WALL CLOCK

Get ready to create a unique and stunning wall clock using epoxy resin. Follow these step-by-step instructions to make your own personalized wall clock.

Necessary materials:

• Transparent epoxy resin

• Hardener for epoxy resin

• Wall clock molds (available online or at craft stores)

• Clock movement with hands (can be purchased online or at watch stores)

• Clock numbers or markers (purchased online or at craft stores)

• Resin-based colors (optional)

• Glitter or other decorative elements (optional)

• Latex gloves

• Mixing rods

• Trowel (or other tool) for removing air bubbles

• Scotch tape

• Scissors

• Brush

Step-by-step instructions:

1. Wear latex gloves to protect your hands when using the resin. Prepare the epoxy following the manufacturer's instructions carefully, mixing the resin and hardener in the correct ratio.

2. If you want to add color to the resin, you can do so using resin-based paints. Add a few drops to the mixture and mix well.

3. You can also spice up the look of the clock by adding glitter or other decorative elements. Mix the elements in the resin carefully.

4. Prepare the mold for the wall clock, making sure it's clean and dry.

5. Pour the prepared epoxy into the mold, filling it to the brim or to the desired amount.

6. If you want to create a layered effect or include decorative elements, you can pour additional layers of resin after allowing the first layer to harden slightly.

7. Follow the instructions that came with the clock movement to position it correctly on the resin surface. Make sure you center it accurately.

8. Press the clock movement down so that it adheres to the resin.

9. Place clock numbers or markers around the edge of the clock. You can use adhesive numbers or apply the markers directly to the resin.

10. Make sure you place the numbers or markers evenly and well spaced out.

11. Use a trowel or scraper tool to gently remove any air bubbles that form on the resin surface. You can tap the surface gently or use a wooden stick to pop the bubbles.

12. Cover the mold with scotch tape to prevent dust or other debris from settling on the surface of the resin as it cures.

13. Allow the resin to cure in the mold for the curing time indicated by the manufacturer's instructions. Usually, this will take several hours or more depending on the type of resin used.

14. Once the resin has fully cured, carefully remove the clock from the mold.

15. Follow the instructions that came with the clock movement to mount the hands on the clock.

16. Place the battery in the clock movement to make it work.

PROJECT 6: COFFEE TABLE

Get ready to transform an ordinary coffee table into a stunning centerpiece with epoxy resin. Follow these step-by-step instructions to create your own resin coffee table.

Necessary materials:

• Raw wood coffee table

• Transparent epoxy resin

• Hardener for epoxy resin

• Resin-based colors (optional)

• Decorative elements such as dried flowers, leaves, shells (optional)

• Latex gloves

• Mixing rods

• Trowel (or other tool) for removing air bubbles

• Scotch tape

• Sandpaper of various grain sizes

• Clear wood sealer (optional)

• Brush

Step-by-step instructions:

1. Get an unfinished wood coffee table and make sure it's clean and free of dust or debris. If necessary, lightly sand the surface of the coffee table to make it smooth and even.

2. Use masking tape to protect any parts of the coffee table that you don't want to cover with resin. For example, you may want to protect the legs or edges of the coffee table.

3. Wear latex gloves to protect your hands when using the resin. Prepare the epoxy following the manufacturer's instructions carefully, mixing the resin and hardener in the correct ratio.

4. If you want to add color to the resin, you can do so using resin-based paints. Add a few drops to the mixture and mix well.

5. Pour the prepared epoxy onto the surface of the coffee table, distributing it evenly. You can create a layered effect or pour the resin over the entire surface, depending on your taste and desired design.

6. Use a trowel to gently remove any air bubbles that form on the surface. You can gently tap the resin with the trowel or use a wooden stick to pop the bubbles.

7. If you want to enrich the look of the coffee table, you can add decorative elements such as dried flowers, leaves, or shells on the resin surface. Position them carefully and lightly press them into the resin to adhere.

8. Use the trowel again to remove any air bubbles that form on the surface after placing the decorative elements.

9. Cover the stage with masking tape to prevent dust or debris from settling on the surface of the resin as it cures.

10. Allow the resin to cure for the curing time indicated by the manufacturer's instructions. Usually, this will take several hours or more depending on the type of resin used.

11. Once the resin has fully cured, remove the tape.

12. If you want a glossy finish, you can apply a clear wood sealer to the surface of the coffee table.

13. If necessary, use sandpaper of various grit sizes to smooth out any roughness or irregularities on the surface of the table.

PROJECT 7: JEWELRY PENDANT

Get ready to create a beautiful and unique resin pendant that reflects your personal style. Follow these step-by-step instructions to make your own resin pendant.

Necessary materials:

• Transparent epoxy resin

• Hardener for epoxy resin

• Blank pendant charm

• Decorative elements such as dried flowers, beads, or leaves (optional)

• Chain or cord for pendant

• Latex gloves

• Mixing rods

• Trowel (or other tool) for removing air bubbles

• Scotch tape

• Sandpaper of various grit sizes

• Scissors

• Brush

Step-by-step instructions:

1. Take the blank pendant and ensure that it is clean and free of any dust or debris. If desired, use fine-grit sandpaper to lightly sand the surface of the pendant, making it smooth and even.

2. Use Scotch tape to protect the parts of the pendant that you don't want to cover with resin. For example, you may want to protect the back or edges of the pendant.

3. Put on latex gloves to protect your hands. Prepare the epoxy by following the manufacturer's instructions, carefully mixing the resin and hardener in the correct ratio.

4. Pour the prepared epoxy into the empty pendant, spreading it evenly. You can choose to fill the pendant completely or create a thin layer, depending on your desired design.

5. Use a trowel or a similar tool to gently remove any air bubbles that form on the resin surface. You can tap the surface gently or use a wooden stick to pop the bubbles.

6. If desired, add decorative elements such as dried flowers, beads, or leaves to the surface of the resin. Position them carefully and lightly press them into the resin to adhere.

7. Use the trowel again to remove any air bubbles that may have formed on the surface after placing the decorative elements.

8. Allow the pendant to cure for the duration specified by the manufacturer's instructions. This typically takes several hours or more, depending on the type of resin used.

9. Once the resin has fully cured, carefully remove the Scotch tape.

10. Use sandpaper of various grit sizes to smooth out any bumps or irregularities on the surface of the pendant. Start with a coarser grit and gradually move to a finer grit for a polished finish.

11. Use scissors to cut a piece of chain or cord to your desired length for the pendant.

12. Pass the chain or cord through the hole in the pendant and secure it with a knot or a small carabiner.

13. Your resin pendant is now ready to be worn and admired!

PROJECT 8: PHOTO HOLDER WITH INCLUDED ELEMENTS

Create a unique and personalized photo holder using epoxy resin and included elements. Follow these step-by-step instructions to make your own photo holder.

Necessary materials:

• Transparent epoxy resin

• Hardener for epoxy resin

• Photo frame or base

• Printed photos or cropped images

• Elements to include such as dried flowers, beads, shells, leaves (optional)

• Latex gloves

• Mixing rods

• Trowel (or other tool) for removing air bubbles

• Scotch tape

• Heat gun (optional)

• Scissors

• Sandpaper of various grain sizes

Step-by-step instructions:

1. Take the photo frame or base that you want to use for the photo holder. Ensure that it is clean and free from any dust or debris.

2. If needed, use fine-grit sandpaper to lightly sand the surface of the frame, making it smooth and even.

3. Use Scotch tape to protect any parts of the frame that you do not want to cover with resin. For example, you may want to protect the edges or the central area where the photo will be placed.

4. Put on latex gloves to protect your hands. Prepare the epoxy resin by following the manufacturer's instructions, carefully mixing the resin and hardener in the correct ratio.

5. Pour the prepared epoxy resin onto the surface of the frame, distributing it evenly. You can choose to fill the entire surface or create a thin layer, depending on your desired design.

6. Use a trowel or a similar tool to gently remove any air bubbles that form on the resin surface. Gently tap the resin with the trowel or use a wooden stick to pop the bubbles. Alternatively, you can use a heat gun to remove the bubbles by briefly passing it over the resin surface.

7. If desired, include elements such as dried flowers, beads, shells, or leaves in the resin to enhance the look of the photo holder. Carefully place them on the resin surface and press them lightly to make them adhere. Use tweezers or a wooden stick to position the items precisely.

8. Use the trowel again to remove any air bubbles that may have formed on the surface after placing the included elements.

9. Allow the resin to cure for the duration specified by the manufacturer's instructions. This typically takes several hours or more, depending on the type of resin used.

10. Once the resin has fully cured, carefully remove the Scotch tape.

11. Use sandpaper of various grain sizes to smooth out any roughness or irregularities on the resin surface. Start with a coarser grit and gradually move to a finer grit for a polished finish.

12. Prepare printed photos or cut-out images of the appropriate size for the frame. Place them in the center of the resin, ensuring they are positioned as desired.

PROJECT 9: LAYERED ABSTRACT PAINTING

Create a captivating layered abstract painting using acrylic paints and epoxy resin. Follow these step-by-step instructions to create your own masterpiece.

Necessary materials:

• Canvas or backing board for painting

• Acrylic paints of different shades

• Spatulas or brushes of various sizes

• Transparent epoxy resin

• Hardener for epoxy resin

• Latex gloves

• Mixing rods

• Trowel (or other tool) for removing air bubbles

• Heat gun (optional)

• Scotch tape

• Transparent protective spray paint

Step-by-step instructions:

1. Prepare your canvas or backing board for painting by ensuring it is clean and free from any dust or debris.

2. Start by creating a base color on your canvas. You can choose a solid color or create a gradient effect using multiple colors. Allow the base layer to dry completely.

3. Prepare your acrylic paints in different shades. Select a darker shade and begin painting thin, transparent layers over the base. Let each layer dry before applying the next to prevent unwanted blending.

4. Continue adding layers of color, gradually moving from darker to lighter shades. This layering technique will create a captivating and dimensional effect.

Experiment with different shapes and directions of strokes to achieve the desired effect.

5. Wear latex gloves to protect your hands when working with epoxy resin.

6. Prepare the epoxy resin according to the manufacturer's instructions, carefully mixing the resin and hardener in the correct ratio.

7. Pour the prepared epoxy resin onto the surface of the painting, ensuring even distribution with a spatula or brush. The resin will add depth and a glossy finish to your artwork.

8. Use a trowel or similar tool to gently remove any air bubbles that may form on the resin surface. You can tap the resin lightly with the trowel or use a wooden stick to pop the bubbles. Alternatively, you can use a heat gun to remove bubbles by briefly passing it over the resin surface.

9. If desired, you can use various tools such as brushes, palette knives, or objects with different textures to create interesting effects on the resin surface. Experiment with creating streaks or dots using a toothpick or brush.

10. Use the trowel again to remove any air bubbles that may have formed on the surface after pouring the resin.

11. Allow the resin to cure for the duration specified by the manufacturer's instructions. This usually takes several hours or more, depending on the type of resin used.

12. Once the resin has fully cured, carefully remove the Scotch tape.

13. To protect your painting and give it a glossy finish, apply a coat of clear protective spray varnish to the surface. Follow the manufacturer's instructions for proper application.

PROJECT 10: DECORATIVE TRAY

Create a stunning decorative resin tray using epoxy resin. Follow these step-by-step instructions to make your own unique piece.

Necessary materials:

- Molds for resin (rectangular or circular molds)
- Transparent epoxy resin
- Hardener for epoxy resin
- Latex gloves
- Mixing rods
- Pigments or dyes for resin (optional)
- Glitter or gold leaf (optional)
- Scotch tape
- Fine grit sandpaper
- Smoothing agent for resin (optional)
- Supports to lift the tray (optional)

Step-by-step instructions:

1. Choose the molds you want to use for creating your decorative resin tray. Ensure that the molds are clean and free from any dust or debris.

2. Wear latex gloves to protect your hands when working with the resin. Prepare the epoxy resin carefully, following the manufacturer's instructions, and mix the resin and hardener in the correct ratio.

3. If desired, add pigments or resin dyes to achieve a specific color for your tray. You can also incorporate glitter or gold leaf for a touch of sparkle and elegance.

4. Pour the prepared epoxy resin into the molds, filling them to the brim or to your desired depth.

5. Use a mixing rod to distribute the resin evenly within the molds.

If you wish to create a marbled effect, gently swirl the colors into the resin using a stick or toothpick.

6. Use a cotton swab or toothpick to remove any air bubbles that may form on the surface of the resin.

7. To achieve a smoother surface, you can use a resin smoothing agent or carefully pass a flame from a lighter or torch over the resin to remove small imperfections. Be cautious and maintain a safe distance to prevent overheating or damage to the resin.

8. Allow the resin to cure for the duration specified by the manufacturer's instructions. This typically takes several hours or more, depending on the type of resin used.

9. Once the resin has fully cured, carefully remove the tray from the molds.

10. Use fine-grit sandpaper to smooth out any bumps or imperfections on the surface of the tray. Take care not to sand too aggressively, as you want to maintain the clarity and shine of the resin.

11. Thoroughly clean the tray to remove any residual resin or dust, ensuring a clean and polished final result.

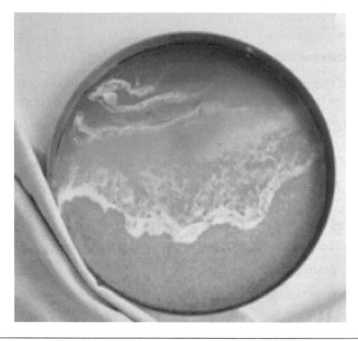

CONCLUSION

We have reached the end of this book that has guided you through the fascinating world of resin art.

We hope you have found inspiration, knowledge, and helpful tips to explore and experiment with this wonderful artistic technique.

Now, it's time to put everything you have learned into practice. Resin art offers endless creative possibilities, allowing you to express your unique vision and create stunning works that reflect your personality and style.

Don't be discouraged by challenges along the way, but see them as opportunities for growth and improvement. With passion, dedication, and creativity, you can create extraordinary works that will leave a lasting impression on the art world.

May your adventure in resin art be filled with inspiration, fulfillment, and surprising discoveries. Explore, experiment, and let your creativity flow without limits!

Great job, and enjoy your artistic journey with resin!

Made in United States
Troutdale, OR
09/20/2023

13064622R00056